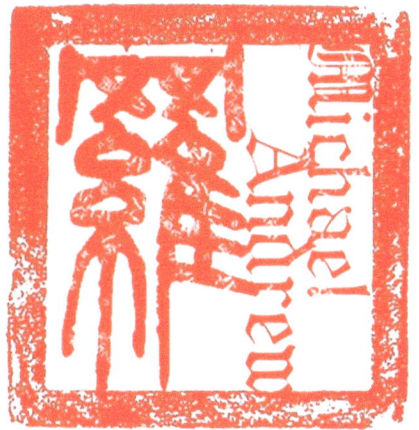

Michael Andrew Law
Visit my website at www.michaelandrewlaw.com

First Printing: 2015
Shop Cheuk Yui

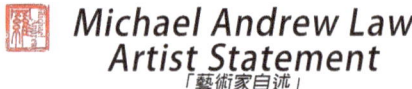

Michael Andrew Law
Artist Statement
「藝術家自述」

My paintings tries to captured the Soul of Youth , I combines classical mediums such as Pigment & Oil with contemporary painting method and medium such as Digital CG as Giclée Prints , I Only interested on ONE but immortal subject matters : Female Figures, by set against the figures with chinese calligraphy Employing the Idea of Word as Image, as an expressive scenario . I use both Life models and Computer Generated Images for the creation of works .

Through juxtaposition, both Icons (The Words and Female figures) , Both added meanings to the other.

These paintings are My Own interpret and to document HongKong's own Millennial and its Generation's view point and identities : As "Hongkonger".

oil on canvas 30x30″

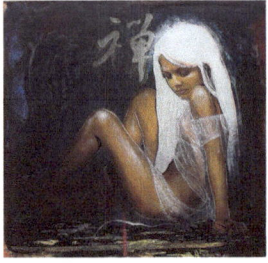

oil on canvas 32x46″

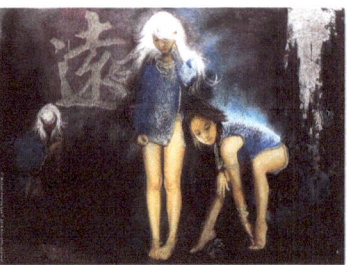

oil on canvas 9x4′

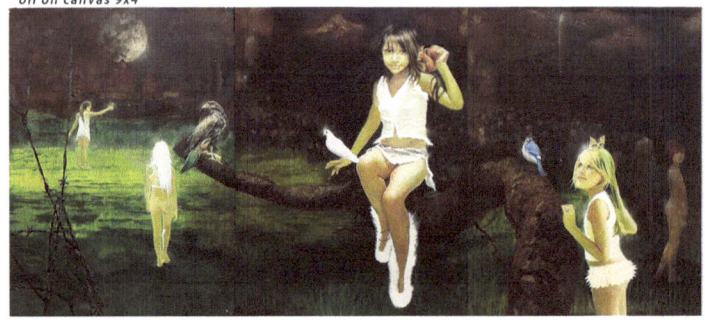

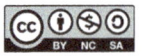

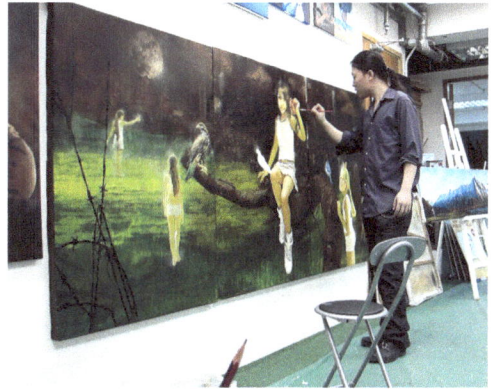

Michael Andrew Law at Work.

Michael Andrew Law

Michael Andrew Law (Born Law Cheuk Yui) was born 1982 in British Hong Kong. After studying Classical oil painting private lessons with New York Artist Daniel Anderson (1928 - 2008) at the his then-new workshop in Hong Kong, he made a stunning reputation as the designer of a number of cover spreads for the press in Hong Kong and abroad and as an illustrator and creative designer of various Comic Books / Story Books .

He then stepped away from commercial work and devoted himself solely to Oil painting. In recent years, he has aesthetically moved away from a stylistic "Icons Photorealist" to HongKonger-Realism, pushing his rendered subjects into a mythological arena. His artistic visions are treasured and collected by many . From there, Law quickly gained recognition in the art world by exhibiting at Hong Kong Convention and Exhibition Centre , The Avenue of Stars ; Law's works are also appreciated and collected by many Hong Kong and international collectors.

Some of Law's Religious artworks for Catholic Church of Hong Kong are also gained media attention in 2006 and 2007 ,and was also received by the Cardinal of the Catholic Church in the same year .

His Pale Hair Girls are a thoroughly subversive tribute to the world of appearances worshipers and to the Hong Kong's Millennial Generation culture of 21 century, with which the painter has cultivated an almost ritualistic relationship. His paintings provoke and compel. There is a unique realness in spirit.

The artist lives and works at Central District , Hong Kong.

Solo Show at NatureArt Gallery

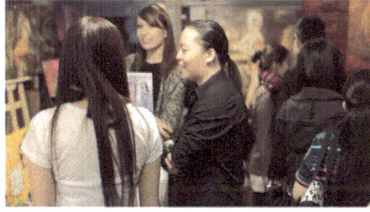

At Ceremony with the Cardinal

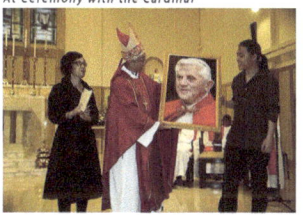

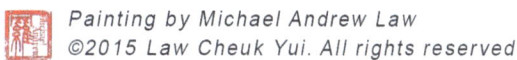
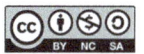

Michael Andrew Law

(852) 6444-7550

info@michaelandrewlaw.com

www.michaelandrewlaw.com

HONORS AND AWARDS:

*Medici Cast Study Recognized by Social Fine Arts Grade Examination Center Of China Academy Of Art.
*Social Fine Arts Grade Examination Center Of China Academy Of Art Promotional Art(2011-present)
Publishers Weekly Best illustrated 's Coffe Book 2004 (Pete M.Parks)
The Salt and The Light Catholic Church Children Book 2004 (Mars)
Borders Magazine Most Original Voices nominee 2006 (Dear Fish)
Publisher's Weekly Best Children's Book list 2004 (America the Beautiful)
Communication Digital Artist -- Award of Excellence
European Print Weekly Design Annual Awards (2000,2002)
Face to face Dolphin art competition silver award 2006
Art Directors of HKC Award of Merit (2005)
Society of Fine Art -- An exhibitor 2005 Society of Newspaper Design Award of Excellence
Michael and Stephanie Duo Exhibition (2006)
Spectrum Fantastic Art Annual (multiple)
not-for-profit aution for Rotary of HK 2012

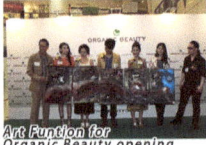
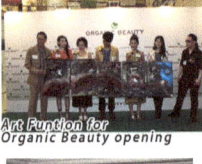

Art Funtion for
Organic Beauty opening

Exhibition :

2013 DeTour Matters 2013 Satellite Events at NatureArt Gallery
2013 December to Remember , One man show at NatureArt Gallery Central District, Hong Kong.
2012 Solo Show , Park Central tseung kwan O ,Hong Kong
2011 Art Walk Group Showing , Discovery Bay ,Hong Kong
2011 HK Gold Coast (Book signing exhibition)
2009 Solo Painting Exhibition The Avenue of Stars
Group Exhibition of Daniel Anderson workshop Classical Realism class of 2008 at Manhattan,NY
2007 Guest and ExhibitionThe Peak Galleria Hong Kong
2007 Invited workshop exhibition, Elements, Hong Kong
Group Exhibition of Classical Realism class of 2007 at Manhattan,NY
2006 Collection by Cardinal Zen Ze-kiun and exhibited at Catholic Church of Hong Kong.
2004 - 2007, Hong Kong Young Artist Group Exhibition, Hong Kong Central Library.
Group Exhibition of Classical Realism class of 2006 at East Village, Manhattan,NY
2005 Illustration original exhibition for Kung Kao Po
2004 Group Exhibition, Wanchai Tower
2003 Group Exhibition, Hong Kong Convention and Exhibition Centre.
2003 Winner of I luv Hong Kong Painting Competition, exhibition at The Landmark (Hong Kong).
2002 The Holy story Picture Book illustrated picture original exhibition ,sai wan ho civic centre.

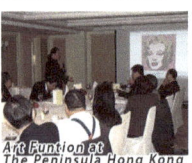

Art Funtion at
The Peninsula Hong Kong

SELECTED COLLECTIONS :

Cardinal of the Catholic Church Joseph Zen Ze-kiun
Organic Beauty Inc
Agriculture, Fisheries and Conservation Department
Ms.Ho Wei Ying
Ms. Annie Yu
Daniel Anderson
MR.Tsang Yan Sam

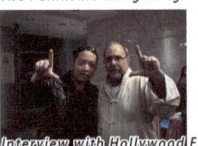

Interview with Hollywood Film
Producer /Teacher Dov Simens

PUBLICATIONS :

Fisheye magazine , featured artist interview , November 2002 (ISBN: N/A)
Kung Kao Po , interview , June 2006 (ISBN: N/A)
Art of Rock Realism , 2008 (ISBN: N/A)
Michael Andrew Law Early works Volume 1 - 3 :
(ISBN-13: 978-1503319400)
(ISBN-13: 978-1503366060)
(ISBN-13: 978-1503365087)
The Pale Hair Girls of Michael Andrew Law , 2010 (ISBN-13: 9781503372115)
December to Remember One man Show Art Book , 2013 (ISBN-13: 9781505609257)
Christmas Everyday : Pale Hair Girls Christmas Series 1 (ISBN-13: 978-1505453218)
Christmas Everyday : Pale Hair Girls Christmas Series 2 (ISBN-13: 978-1505467796)
Christmas Everyday : Pale Hair Girls Christmas Series 3 (ISBN-13: 978-1505468052)
Christmas Everyday : Pale Hair Girls Christmas Series 4 (ISBN-13: 978-1505470741)
Christmas Everyday : Pale Hair Girls Christmas Series 5 (ISBN-13: 978-1505470857)
Christmas Everyday : Pale Hair Girls Christmas Series 6 (ISBN-13: 978-1505471151)
Christmas Everyday : Pale Hair Girls Christmas Series Specials (ISBN-13: 978-1505583922)
i-Egoism by Michael Andrew Law (ISBN:978-1-4990-2124-0)

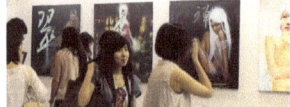

Exhibition at
Hong Kong Central Library.

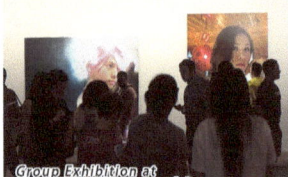

Group Exhibition at
Hong Kong Museum of Art

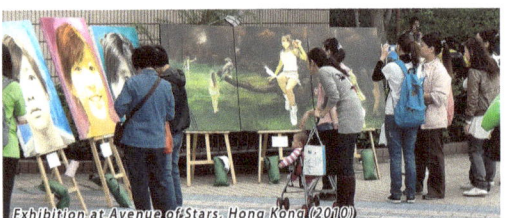

Exhibition at Avenue of Stars, Hong Kong (2010)

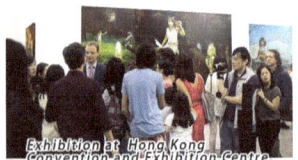

Exhibition at Hong Kong
Convention and Exhibition Centre.

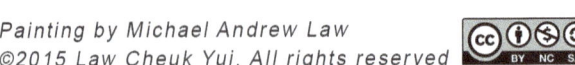

關 於藝術家MICHAEL ANDREW LAW:

生長於交接時期香港的年輕藝術家 Michael Andrew Law，擅長把數碼繪圖，Pop 摩登藝術及古典油畫揉合時事及諷刺，創出獨特的視覺藝術語言及內容，跨越中西混合背景思維界限，探索互聯網世代交錯回歸的中西混雜之香港歷史。

他以自由隨意的手法結合摩登及古典材料與技巧，保持表現與認知、控制與隨性、魯莽與機智、自我與社群等對立美學力量之間的張力，並對香港Y世代、本土文化及民族社會的殘酷現實作出尖刻的評論。Michael Andrew Law 的作品色彩豐富，寫實風格描繪的冰山美人，刻畫在滿佈流行文化圖像、東方書法標誌及符號的背景上。《白髮女孩系列》(The Pale Hair Girls，2006 — 2013 年) 的創作之中，Michael Andrew Law 獨特的繪畫風格呈獻出達達主義思考方式般的且出人意表的效果。畫中冰山美人式的人物穿插在抽象的香港和俗世符號上。

Pale Hair Girls系列的畫作的視覺靈感大量源自法國美術學院派大師William-Adolphe Bouguereau 的少年油畫作品以及已故華裔畫家陳逸飛的史詩及美人作品，Michael Andrew Law一反傳統的繪畫技法，以數碼混合古典繪畫技，重新演繹細緻複雜的中西方古典畫面和精心細思考的構圖，以西式媒介呼應中國的傳統書法作代為圖案之筆觸，在Michael Andrew Law的筆下這種交錯西式POP ART和中式古典藝術表現時輪廓卻非常細緻，尤其最廣為流傳和臨摹的Leonardo da Vinci作品Mona Lisa (1517 年)，以東方血統之妻子肖像取代Mona Lisa 的表徵意義，極具質感的厚顏料同現寫生畫作時人物肉體的細微變化。

《誰會理會不是自已的新天地:三聯畫》(Humanity) 刻畫了在世代末日的未來世代們於本為廢墟的香港島上，等待著他們的命運。這些離奇的場景與Jerry B. Jenkins及Timothy LaHaye等當代作家描寫的超現實、宗教解讀、未來主義情懷如出一致。於半島酒店扶輪會演講當代藝術

主要探索他藝術裡其中一項最重要的二分法：浪漫與嘲諷、作為藝術家對美的浪漫思考與交滙中西混合背景思維之香港Y世代的悲情，由天真燦爛的冰山美人式少女與可怕的末日和俗物之間的強烈對比作象徵。無論是標誌性的單幅「古典書法圖案的無身份肖像」，抑或以三聯畫形式出現，運用到大師極繪畫與構圖技巧，揉合了精細傳統油畫技法與摩登畫的表現方式建構，美人亦在美術史和流行文化裡是永恆的主題。冰山美人式少女令人聯想到生命的脆弱與時光飛逝之無情。藝術家就是要了解不同世界之間的界線並翻譯到不同文化價值之間的語境如高尚對低俗、古代對現代、東方對西方。

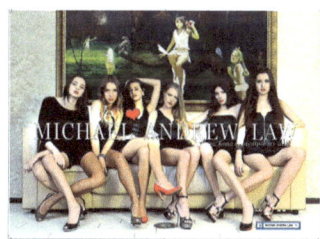
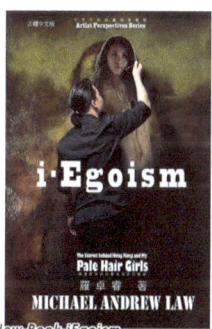

New Book iEgoism
ISBN:978-1-4990-2124-0

憑著 iEgoism 故事性的風格和精神，Michael Andrew Law將流行、古典與時事內容混合成一種感覺超豐富的視覺藝術作品，所涉獵的美學領域和文化靈感不斷延伸，而他在當中游走自如。一如常見的當代藝術主題，去作為「諷刺」及「反思」有關「浪漫」與「悲情」的直接敘述。

他所開發的iEgoism主題，就深受當代或反傳統藝術愛好者的喜愛，這被視為跟西方DADA藝術主義互相呼應。Michael Andrew Law把自己置身於他熱烈的自我網世代主義- iEgoism裡展現出的姿態卻是完全屬於他本人和他的時代的。

Michael Andrew Law於2006 年隨美國紐約藝術家Daniel Anderson深造古典油畫，其後發展純美術繪畫工作，2008年獲贊助於香港中環成立藝術工作室 Nature Art。除了製作藝術及相關作品，Nature Art 及 Michael Andrew Law 亦積極培育香港年輕藝術家。

2013 年，他於NatureArt Gallery舉行藝術展覽《iEgoism》，從香港歷史中追溯當代香港流行視覺藝術文化的特徵。

Michael Andrew Law 的作品曾於紐約 Chelsea 的聯合展覽中展出，他亦曾在著名機構及學校舉行個展及講座，例如星光大道 (2009 年)、天主教香港教區、香港中央圖書館(2004 -2007 年)、灣仔政府大樓外(2004 年)、香港會議展覽中心 (2003 年)。2015出版藝術文字著作《不可不知的藝術家觀點系列-iEgoism》更深入探討香港Y世代、香港歷史和Michael Andrew Law的作品脈絡關聯。

Michael Andrew Law 現於香港定居及從事創作。

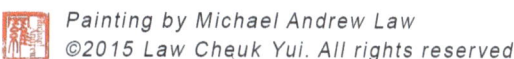
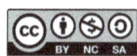

Michael Andrew Law fusing digital and classical painting with west and East creative philosophy , to produce an extremely original artistic language and content that bridged west and east ,classical and modern medium , at the same time clearly tells the stories of his own generation. Combining digital creative materials and classical painting techniques with effusive yet knowing and precise focused , his paintings maintain a powerful tension between opposing aesthetic forces—expression and knowledge, control and spontaneity, savagery and wit, urbanity and primitivism—while providing satiric commentary on the oppressive realities of the predicament of Generation Internet, homegrown hongkonger's local-culture vesus Traditional Chinese culture, and The Hong Kong's post-handover history.

In his dynamically designed compositions, gracefully detailed figures and innocent faces are incise against fields that juxtaposed with portraits, chinese calligraphy, and sometimes cgi. The Pale Hair Girls Series (2006 - 2013) depicts realistic cold, icy-like young female figures surrounded by abstract and expressively painted forms and shapes revealing images of Pop culture, Historial figures, and Hong Kong landmarks.

Michael Andrew Law draws inspiration from Old Master's works such as Caravaggio , Ruben , Rembrandt , all the way to the Modern Art Superstars such as Warhol , Lichtenstein , Richter , De Kooning , Bacon , Wool and Prince . The Pale Hair Girls series mainly inspired by the painting works of French academic painter and traditionalist William-Adolphe Bouguereau and the Late Great YiFei Chen's characteristic "Romantic Realism" paintings.

In a reversal of standard East-West aesthetics, Law re-interprets Old Master's sophisticated imagery combine classical and digital materials—which resonate with Digital Vector Designs and Paintings—with fine strokes of oil paint multi-layered with paint film.In his interpretation of Leonardo Da Vinci's iconic Mona Lisa's smile (1517)—an iconic image that has been endlessly disseminated and reproduced—Law painted over the symbolism of the portrait Mona Lisa with his young wife , intent on rendering the figure in contemporary fashion with the iconic image as background .

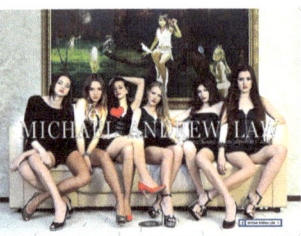

New Book IEgoism
ISBN:978-1-4990-2124-0

"The Humanity triptych" depicts New Generation HongKongers in a Ruined Hong Kong city , awaiting their unknown fate of a new beginning. This painting series explores one of the central paradox of his art—between romance and derision , his romantic magnanimity as an artist and his pessimistic perspective on the predicament of Generation Y Hongkongers. Here, this paradox is symbolized by the stark contrast of icy cold young female and disturbing representations of the armageddon-like of images. Whether portrayed as single "chinese calligraphy " or in triptych composition and classical paintwork that combine both expressive and traditional painting techniques with the digital vector , the beauties and the human figures stand as eternal motifs in the history of art and also in popular culture. Both oppositional and parallel, they are reminders of the fragile vibrancy of life and the impitoyable passing of time.

A references between different cultural refrence (high/pop, classical/contemporary, east/west), Michael Andrew Law has stated that an artist should be someone who understood how to hybrid between different worlds and go ahead makes an effort to knowing them. With his distinctive "iEgoism" philosophy , which employs highly refined academic painting techniques to depict a mixture of abstract expressionism within a representational pop culture images. These techniques parallel to the themes of romance and predicament of this generation , he recollects and revitalizes narratives of irony and introspection.

Michael Andrew Lawwas born in 1982 in British Hong Kong , studied fine art with american artist Daniel Anderson and graduate of China Central Academy of Fine Arts Sam Zeng from 2003 - 2006 . He co-founded the Hong Kong Art Studio Nature Art Workshop in 2008. In addition to the production and marketing of Michael Andrew Law's art and related work, Nature Art functions as a supportive environment for the fostering of emerging Hong Konger artists. Law is also a curator. In 2013, he organized an exhibition of contemporary art titled "iEgoism ," which served as a narration of contemporary HongKong Gen Y pop culture .

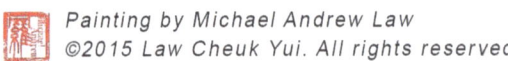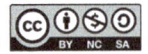

Michael Andrew Law

(852) 6444-7550
info@michaelandrewlaw.com
www.michaelandrewlaw.com

Selected publications

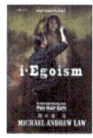

iEgoism by Michael Andrew Law
Softcover : 110 pages
Publisher : Xlibris LLC
ISBN: Softcover 978-1-4990-2124-0
ISBN: EBook 978-1-4990-2118-9

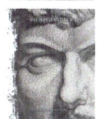

Michael Andrew Law The early years volume one: Nine Drawings from the early years collection
ISBN-10: 1503319407
ISBN-13: 978-1503319400

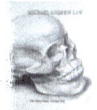

Michael Andrew Law The early years volume Two: Nine more Drawings from the early years collection (Volume 2)
ISBN-10: 1503365085
ISBN-13: 978-1503365087

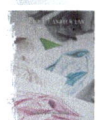

Michael Andrew Law The early years volume Three: Nine Drawings from the early years collection (Volume 3)
ISBN-10: 1503366065
ISBN-13: 978-1503366060
Product Dimensions: 6 x 0.1 x 9 inches

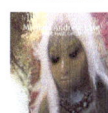

Michael Andrew Law: Pale Hair Girls Catalogue (Volume 1)
Paperback: 124 pages
ISBN-10: 1503372111
ISBN-13: 978-1503372115
Product Dimensions: 8.5 x 0.3 x 8.5 inches

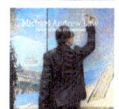

December To Remember: Michael Andrew Law Exhibition
Paperback: 120 pages
ISBN-10: 1505609259
ISBN-13: 978-1505609257

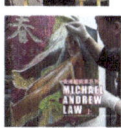

Hong Kong Artist Series: Michael Andrew Law 1
Paperback: 48 pages
ISBN-10: 1507580665
ISBN-13: 978-1507580660

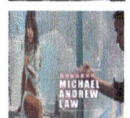

Hong Kong Artist Series: Michael Andrew Law 2'
Paperback: 48 pages
ISBN-10: 1507581556
ISBN-13: 978-1507581551

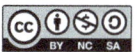

Michael Andrew Law

(852) 6444-7550
info@michaelandrewlaw.com
www.michaelandrewlaw.com

Publications : Illustrated Books

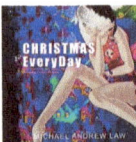

Christmas Everyday Book 1: Pale Hair Girls Christmas Series (Pale Hair Girls Christmas Everyday) (Volume 1)
ISBN-10: 1505453216
ISBN-13: 978-1505453218
Product Dimensions: 8.5 x 0.1 x 8.5 inches

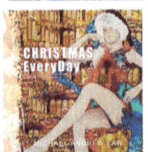

Christmas Everyday Book 2: Pale Hair Girls Christmas Series (Pale Hair Girls Christmas Everyday) (Volume 2)
ISBN-10: 1505467799
ISBN-13: 978-1505467796
Product Dimensions: 8.5 x 0.1 x 8.5 inches

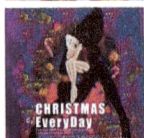

Christmas Everyday Book 3: Pale Hair Girls Christmas Series (Pale Hair Girls Christmas Everyday) (Volume 3)
ISBN-10: 1505468051
ISBN-13: 978-1505468052
Product Dimensions: 8.5 x 0.1 x 8.5 inches

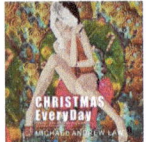

Christmas Everyday Book 4: Pale Hair Girls Christmas Series (Pale Hair Girls Christmas Everyday) (Volume 4)
ISBN-10: 1505470749
ISBN-13: 978-1505470741
Product Dimensions: 8.5 x 0.1 x 8.5 inches

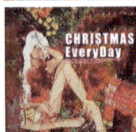

Christmas Everyday Book 5: Pale Hair Girls Christmas Series (Pale Hair Girls Christmas Everyday) (Volume 5)
ISBN-10: 1505470854
ISBN-13: 978-1505470857
Product Dimensions: 8.5 x 0.1 x 8.5 inches

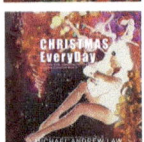

Christmas Everyday Book 6: Pale Hair Girls Christmas Series (Pale Hair Girls Christmas Everyday) (Volume 6)
ISBN-10: 150547115X
ISBN-13: 978-1505471151
Product Dimensions: 8.5 x 0.1 x 8.5 inches

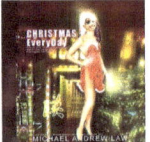

Christmas Everyday: Special Edition (Pale Hair Girls Christmas Everyday) (Volume 7)
ISBN-10: 1505583926
ISBN-13: 978-1505583922
Product Dimensions: 8.5 x 0.3 x 8.5 inches

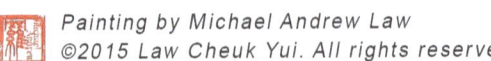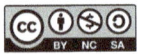

Michael Andrew Law

(852) 6444-7550
info@michaelandrewlaw.com
www.michaelandrewlaw.com

Selected Works for Art Events

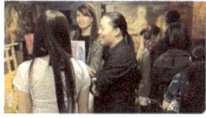

iEgoism Exhibition at NatureArt ,Central District Hong Kong

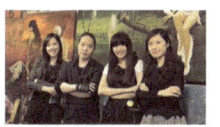

iEgoism Exhibition In Photos (from left) : TV/ Movie stars Cherrie Kong ,Michael Andrew Law , Iva law ,Florence Lawman.

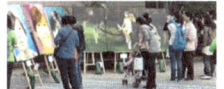

Michael Andrew Law exhibition at the Avenue of Stars, Hong Kong (星光大道).

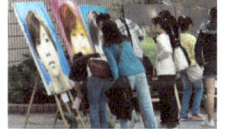

Michael Andrew Law exhibition at the Avenue of Stars, Hong Kong (星光大道).

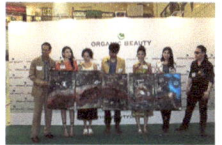

Art Related Events for Organic Beauty opening,

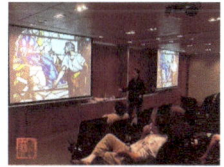

Art Talks at Credit Agricole CIB, Hong Kong Branch

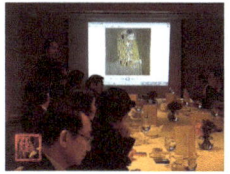

Art Talks for The Rotary Club of Hong Kong At The Peninsula Hong Kong

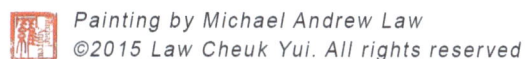
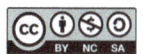

Michael Andrew Law

(852) 6444-7550
info@michaelandrewlaw.com
www.michaelandrewlaw.com

Selected Works for Art Events

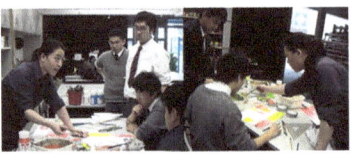

As Guest Art Tutor at Diocesan Boys' School

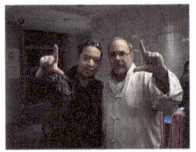

Working With Film Producer & Founder of Hollywood Film Institute Dov Simens.

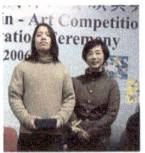

Art Competition Award ceremony with Dr. Sarah Mary Liao , then-Secretary for the Environment of the Hong Kong Special Administrative Region .

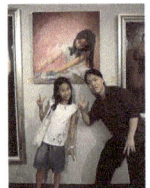

Self Curated Exhibition with Art Collectors at Art Center ,2005.

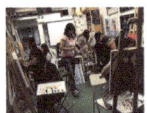

Curated Art Events with The Swire Group (太古集團).

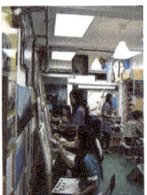

Curated Art Events with Hong Kong Stock Exchange (香港交易所).

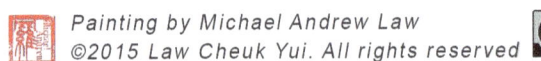
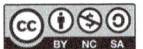

Michael Andrew Law

(852) 6444-7550
info@michaelandrewlaw.com
www.michaelandrewlaw.com

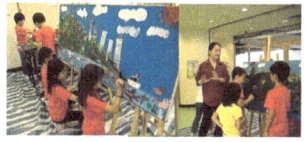

Art Event with Young Men's Christian Association (YMCA).

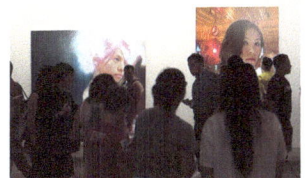

Group Exhibition, Hong Kong Convention and Exhibition Centre.

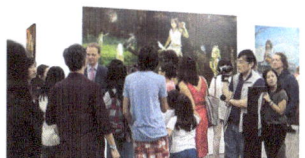

iEgoism Exhibition

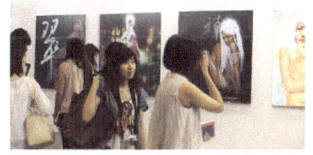

Exhibition, Elements, Hong Kong

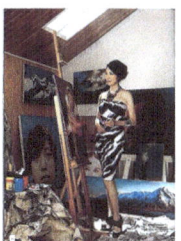

Oil Painting Shown in magazine :
壹周刊第1047期]第20屆壹電視大獎 – 謝雪心

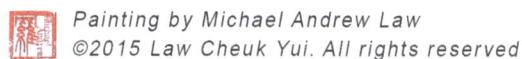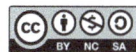

Michael Andrew Law

(852) 6444-7550
info@michaelandrewlaw.com
www.michaelandrewlaw.com

Selected Works for Art Events

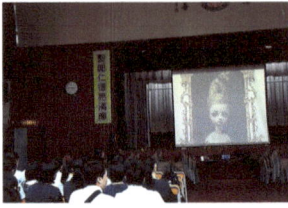

Art Talk and Exhibition at Pui Shing Catholic Secondary School.

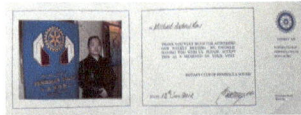

Art Talks and Charity Auction for The Rotary Club of Hong Kong At The Peninsula Hong Kong

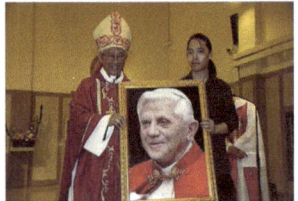

Cardinal Zen Ze-kiun receives Michael Andrew Law at Ceremony. Comission portrait by Catholic Church of Hong Kong

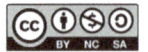

Michael Andrew Law

(852) 6444-7550
info@michaelandrewlaw.com
www.michaelandrewlaw.com

The Pale Hair Universe Series

Medium : Traditional Oil Painting (With Acrylic Based) , Glitter , Gold Leaf .
About This Serie : Created Along with the First Series of painting of The Pale Hair Girls Original Series Paintings , Done with mixed media on canvas , with classical painting method.
Number of Paintings : 7 (As of 2015)
Availability : Limited Edition , Prints , Original Painting

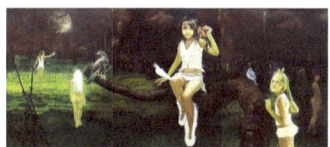

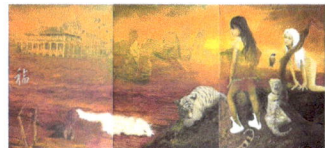

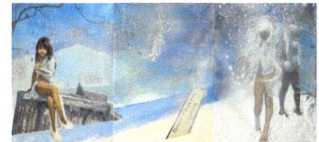

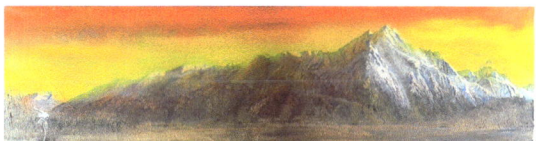

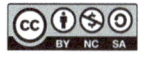

Michael Andrew Law

(852) 6444-7550
info@michaelandrewlaw.com
www.michaelandrewlaw.com

Pale Hair Girls Original Series.

Medium : Traditional Oil Painting (With Acrylic Based) , Glitter , Gold Leaf .
About This Serie : First Series of painting of The entire Pale Hair Girls Universe ,
done with mixed media on canvas , with classical painting method.
Number of Paintings : 60 (As of 2015)
Availability : Limited Edition , Prints , Original Painting

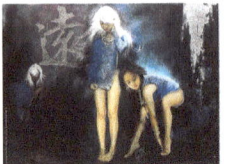 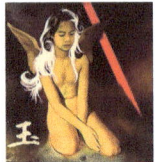 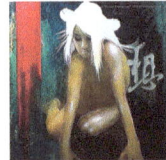 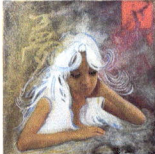

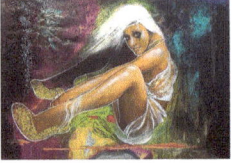 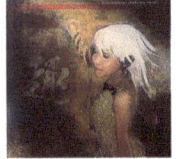 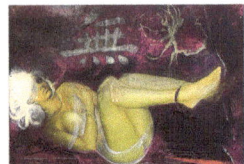

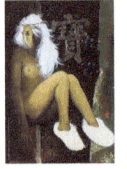 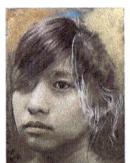 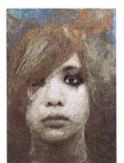 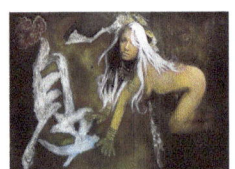

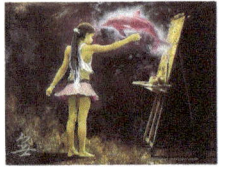 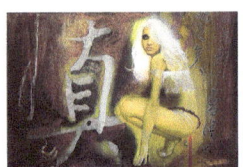 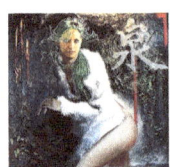

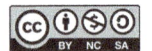

Details

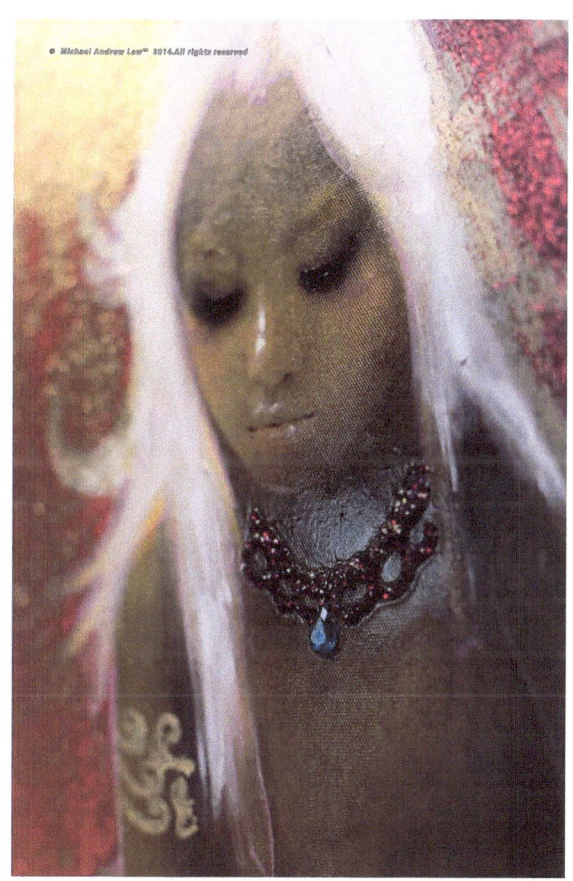

info@michaelandrewlaw.com
www.michaelandrewlaw.com

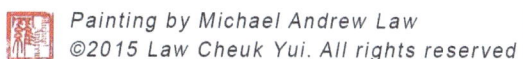 *Painting by Michael Andrew Law*
 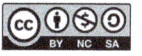

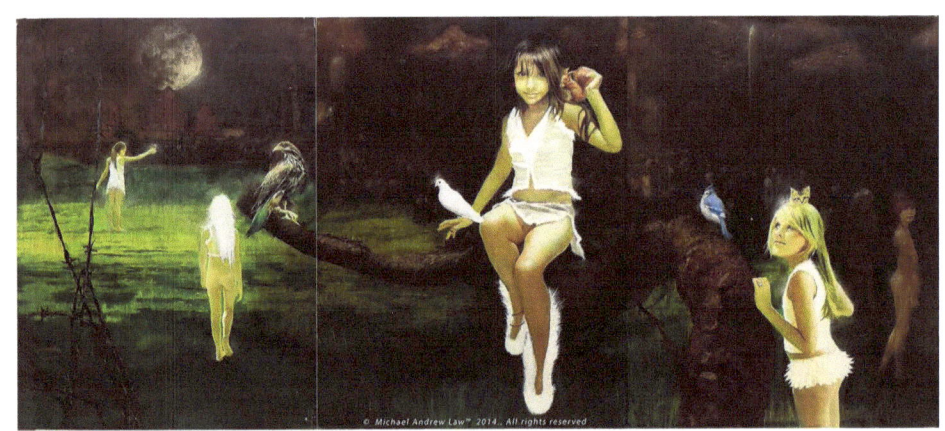

4'x 9' Multi-Panel Painting

info@michaelandrewlaw.com
www.michaelandrewlaw.com

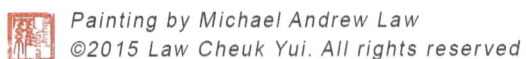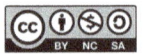

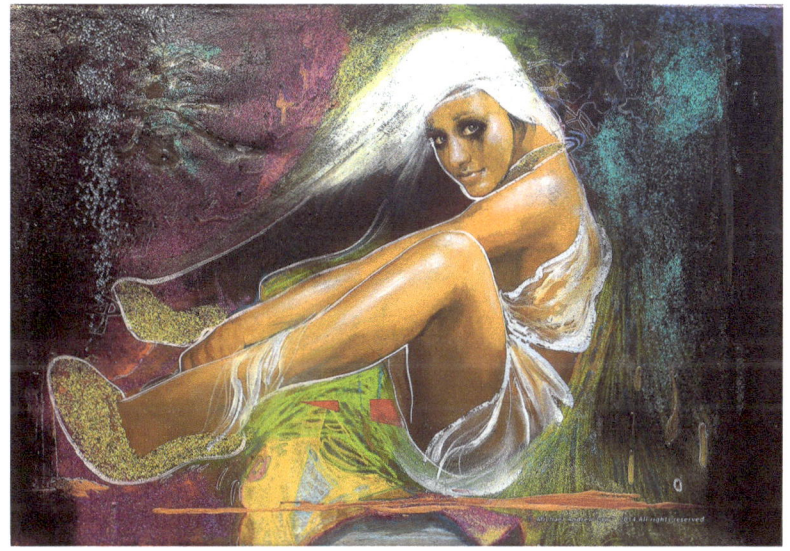

30x20 ″ oil on canvas

S-P-R-I-N-G

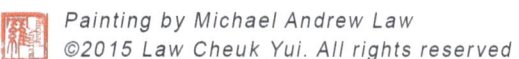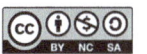

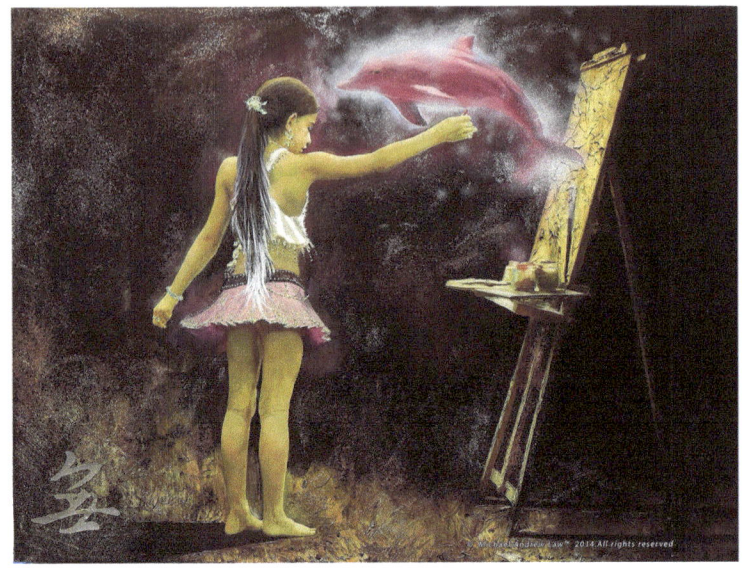

48x36 " oil on canvas

Nothing stops dreams

info@michaelandrewlaw.com
www.michaelandrewlaw.com

© Michael Andrew Law™ 2014.All rights reserved

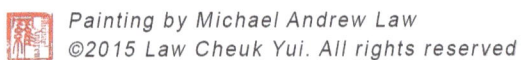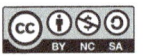

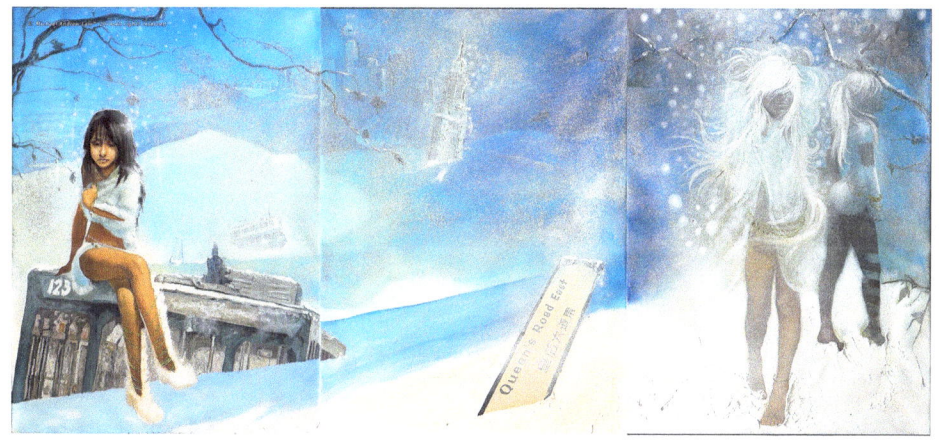

4'x 9' Multi-Panel Painting

info@michaelandrewlaw.com
www.michaelandrewlaw.com

© Michael Andrew Law™ 2014.All rights reserved

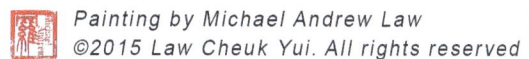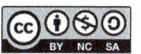

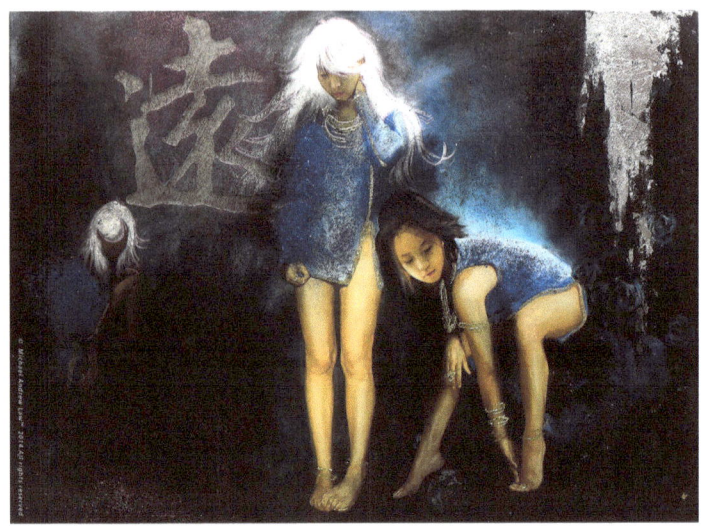

32x46 ˝ oil on canvas

Somewhere beyond my reach

info@michaelandrewlaw.com
www.michaelandrewlaw.com

© Michael Andrew Law™ 2014.All rights reserved

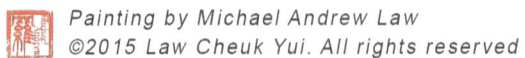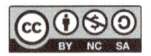

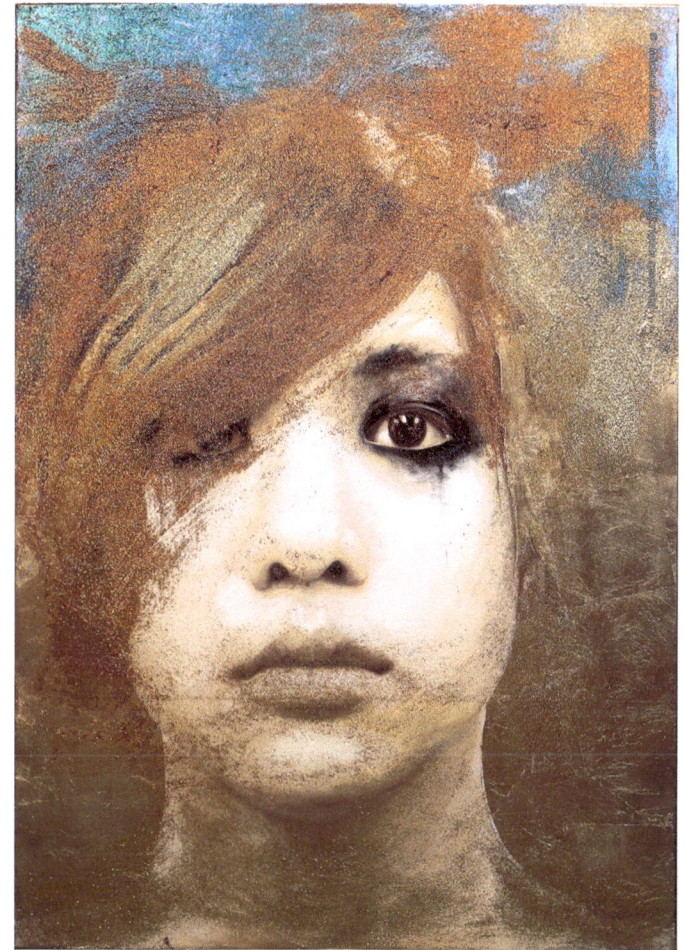

36x48 ˝ oil on canvas

Goodbye Future II

info@michaelandrewlaw.com
www.michaelandrewlaw.com

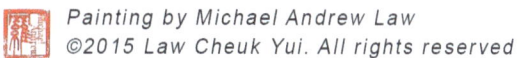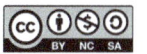

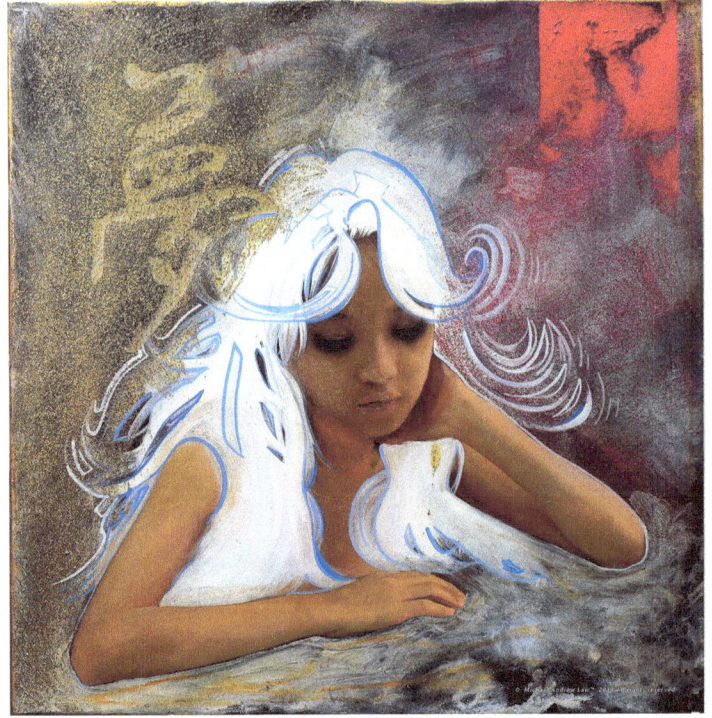

30x30 " oil on canvas

I only dreams cause I am Alive.

info@michaelandrewlaw.com
www.michaelandrewlaw.com

© Michael Andrew Law™ 2014.All rights reserved

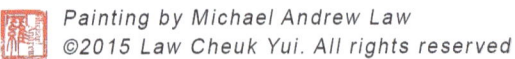
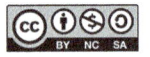

Michael Andrew Law

(852) 6444-7550
info@michaelandrewlaw.com
www.michaelandrewlaw.com

Pale Hair Girls : The New

Medium : Mixed Media Painting (oil and Acrylic) , Glitter , Gold Leaf .
About This Serie : Second Series of painting of The entire Pale Hair Girls Universe ,
done with mixed media on canvas , classical method crossover with contemporary Digital painting method.
Number of Paintings : 80 (As of 2015)
Availability : Limited Edition , Prints , Special Edition .

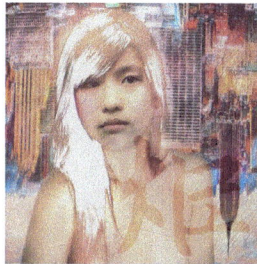
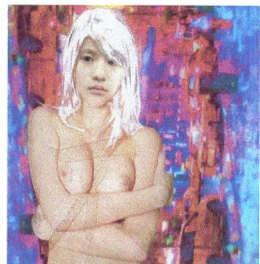
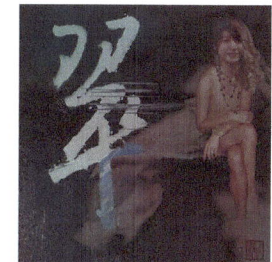

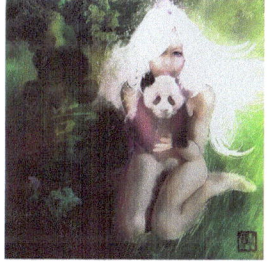
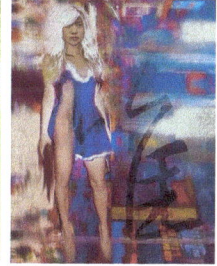
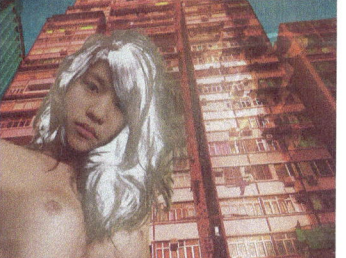

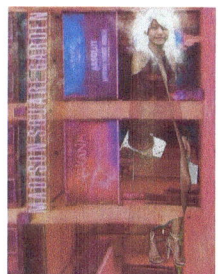
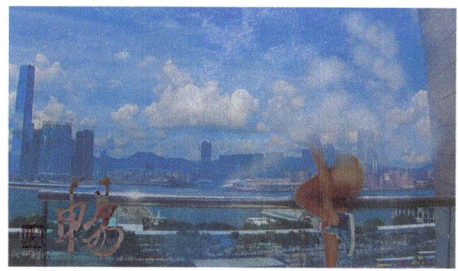

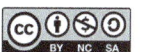

Michael Andrew Law

(852) 6444-7550
info@michaelandrewlaw.com
www.michaelandrewlaw.com

Pale Hair Girls : The New

Medium : Mixed Media Painting (oil and Acrylic) , Glitter , Gold Leaf .
About This Serie : Second Series of painting of The entire Pale Hair Girls Universe , done with mixed media on canvas , classical method crossover with contemporary Digital painting method.
Number of Paintings : 80 (As of 2015)
Availability : Limited Edition , Prints , Special Edition .

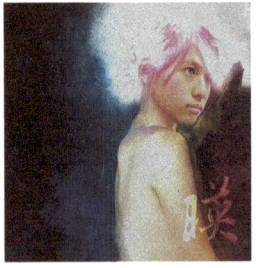 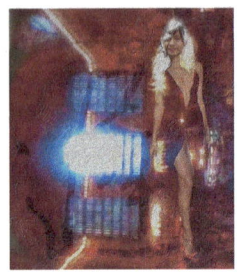 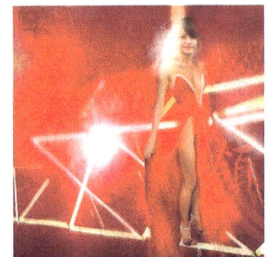

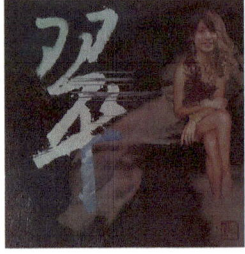 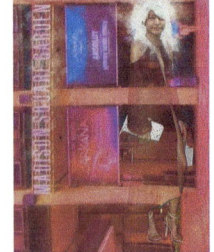 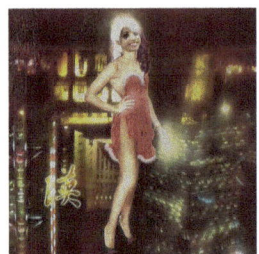

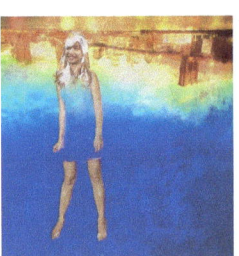 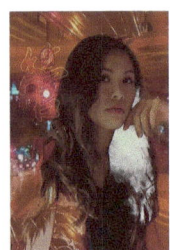 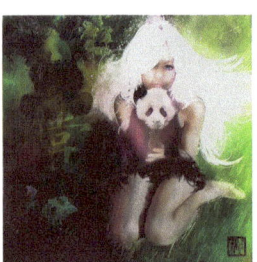

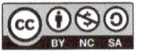

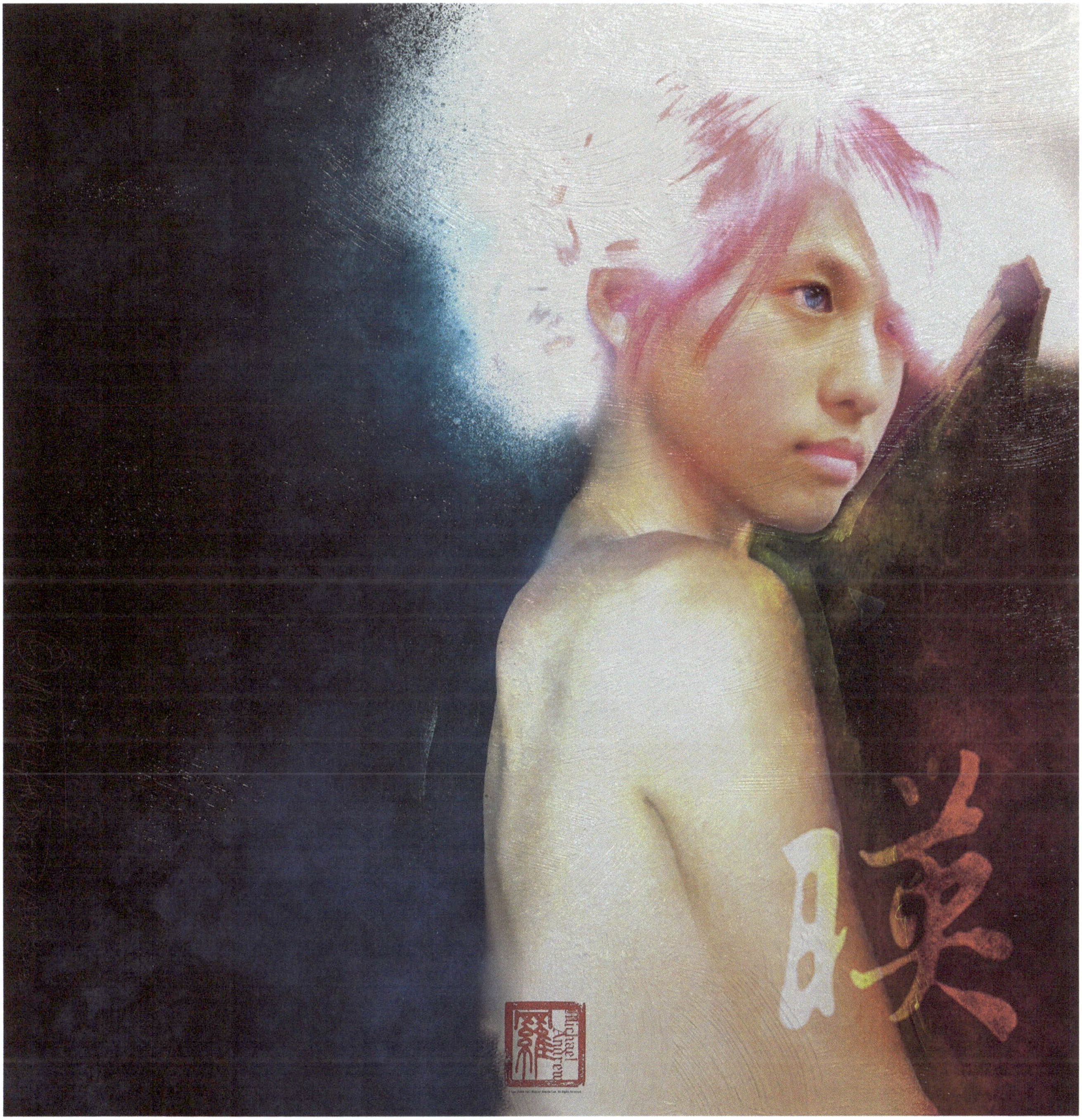

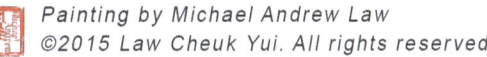

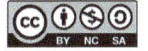

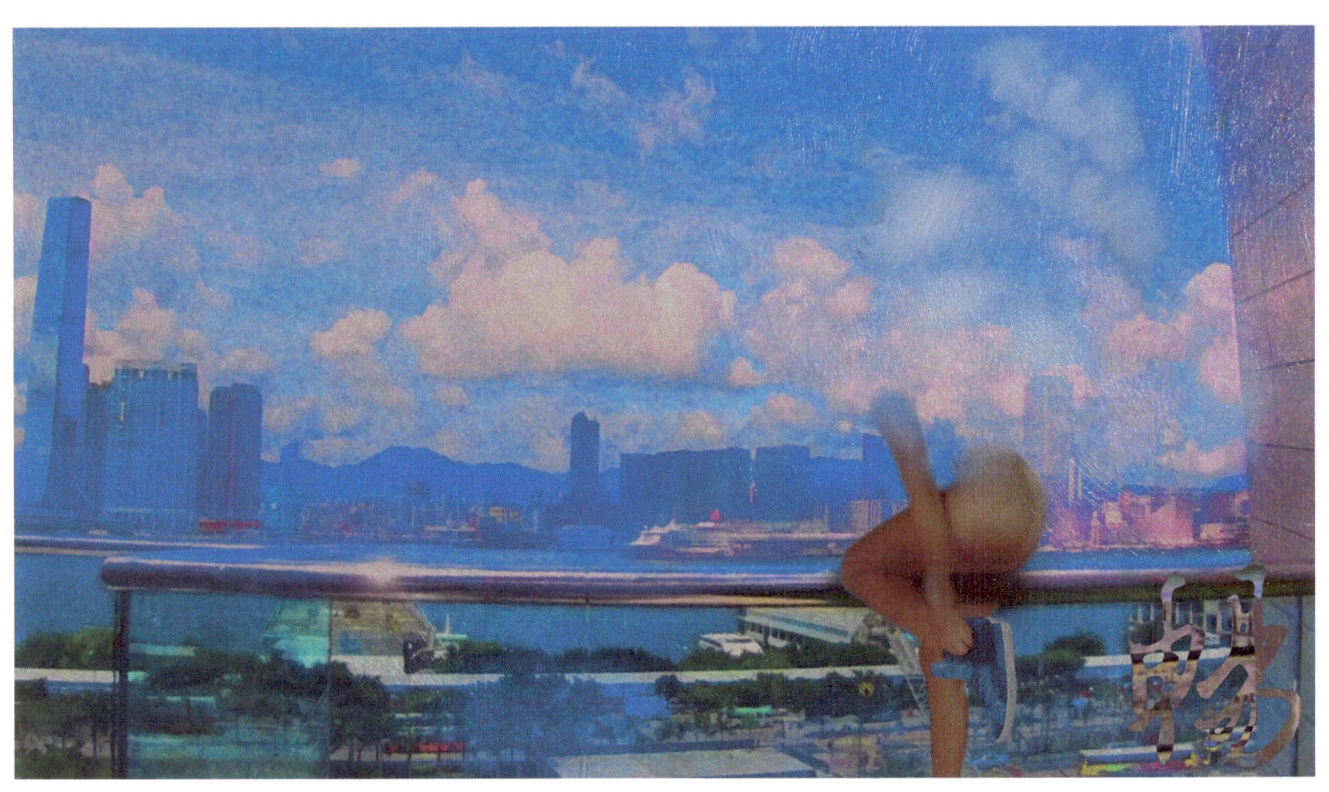

Michael Andrew Law

(852) 6444-7550
info@michaelandrewlaw.com
www.michaelandrewlaw.com

Pale Hair Girls : Christmas Everyday

Medium : Mixed Media Painting (digital print with Acrylic) , Glitter , Gold Leaf .
About This Serie : Special Series illustrations of The Pale Hair Girls Universe ,
done with mixed media on canvas , classical method crossover with contemporary Digital
painting method.
Number of Paintings : 102 (As of 2015)
Availability : Limited Edition , Prints , Special Edition .

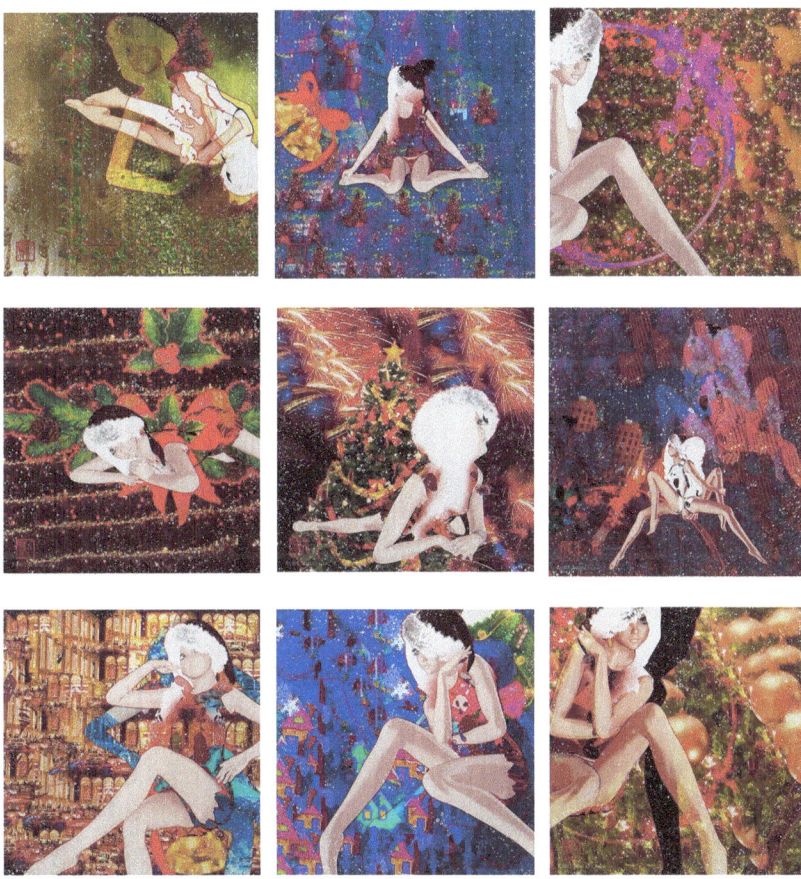

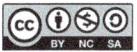

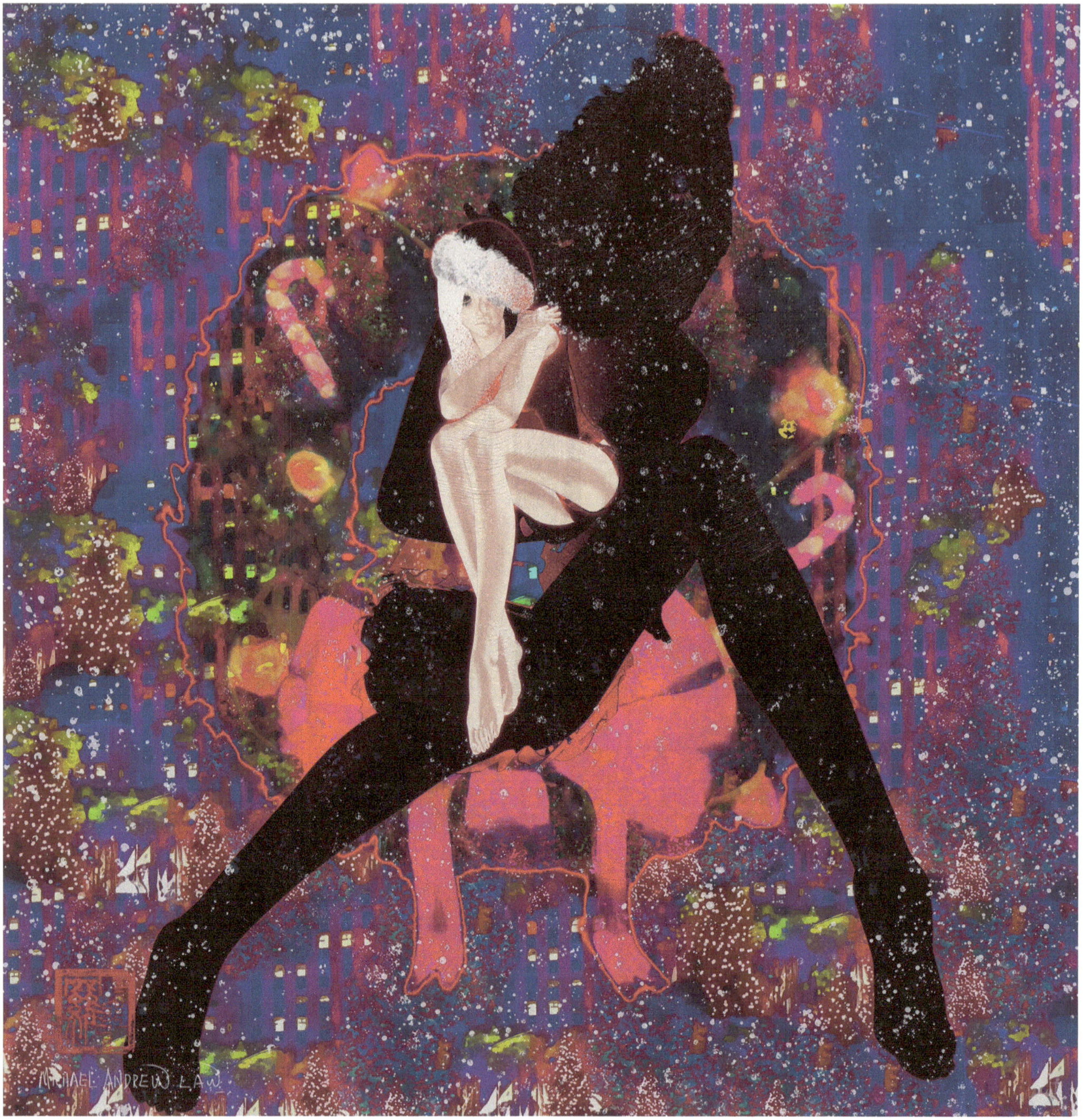

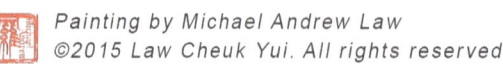

Forgive the guilty.

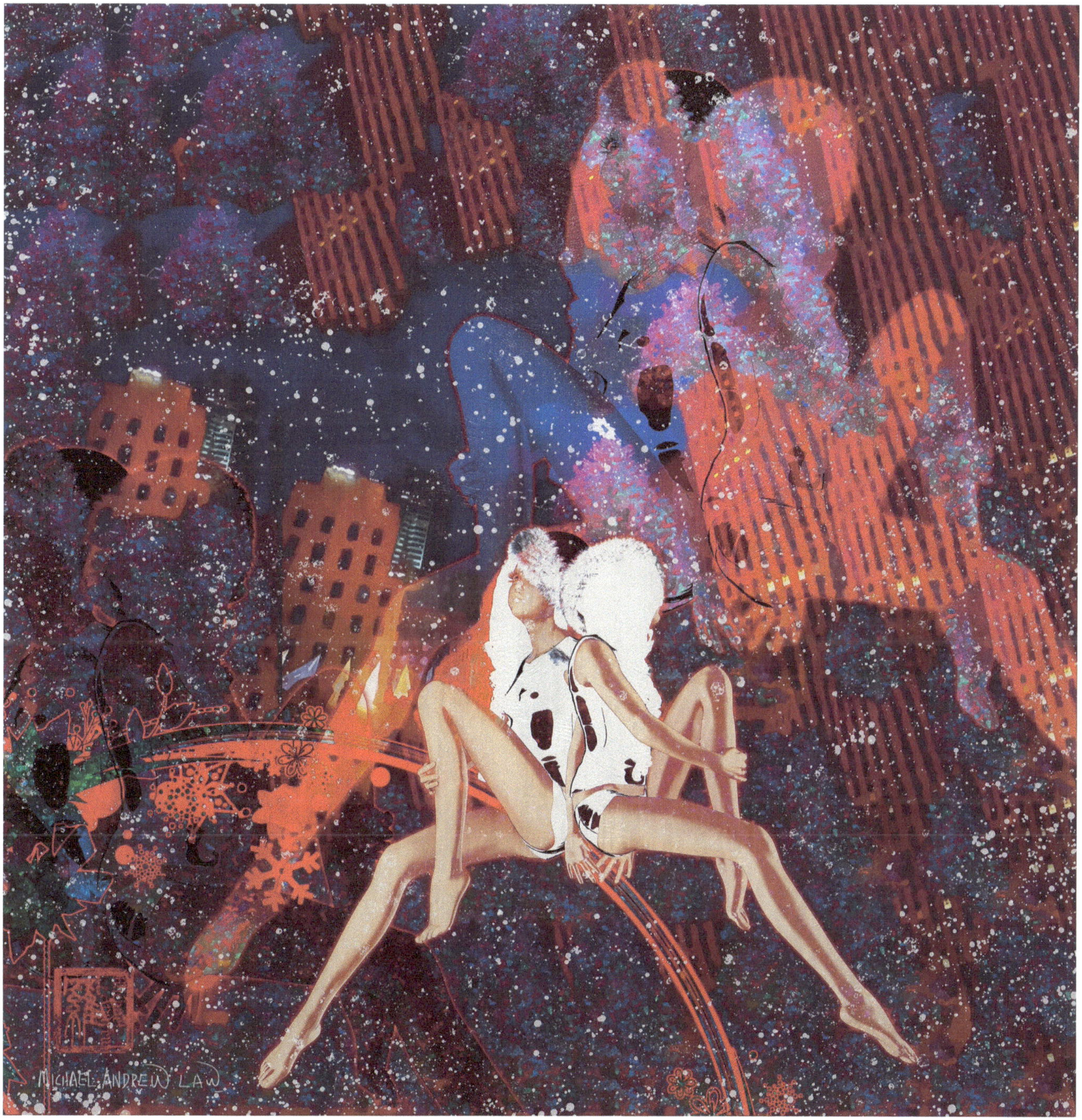

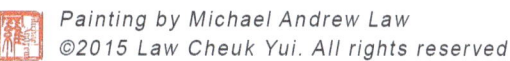

am I allowed to go Christmas shopping?

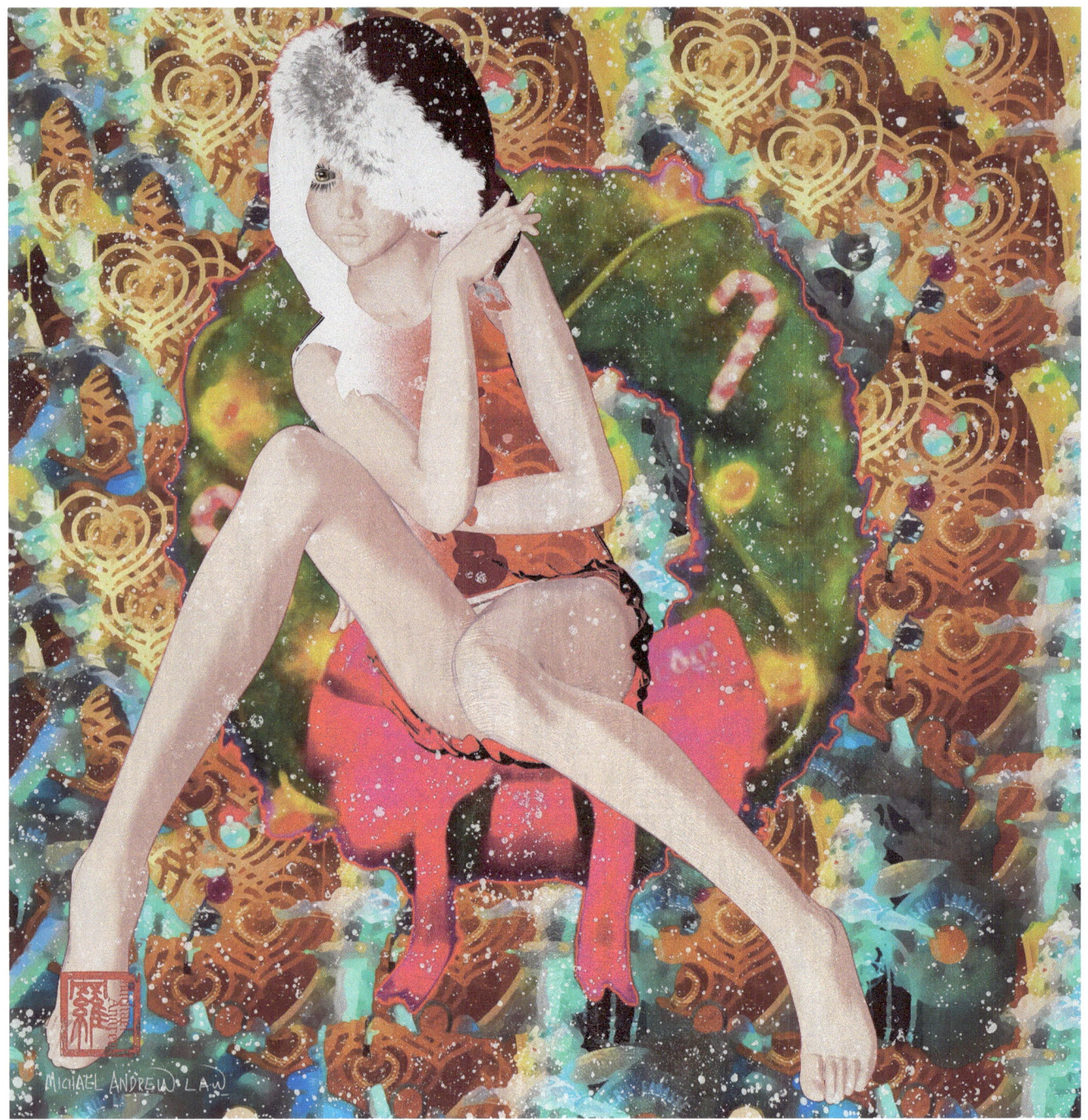

Peace on earth will come to stay, when we live Christmas every day

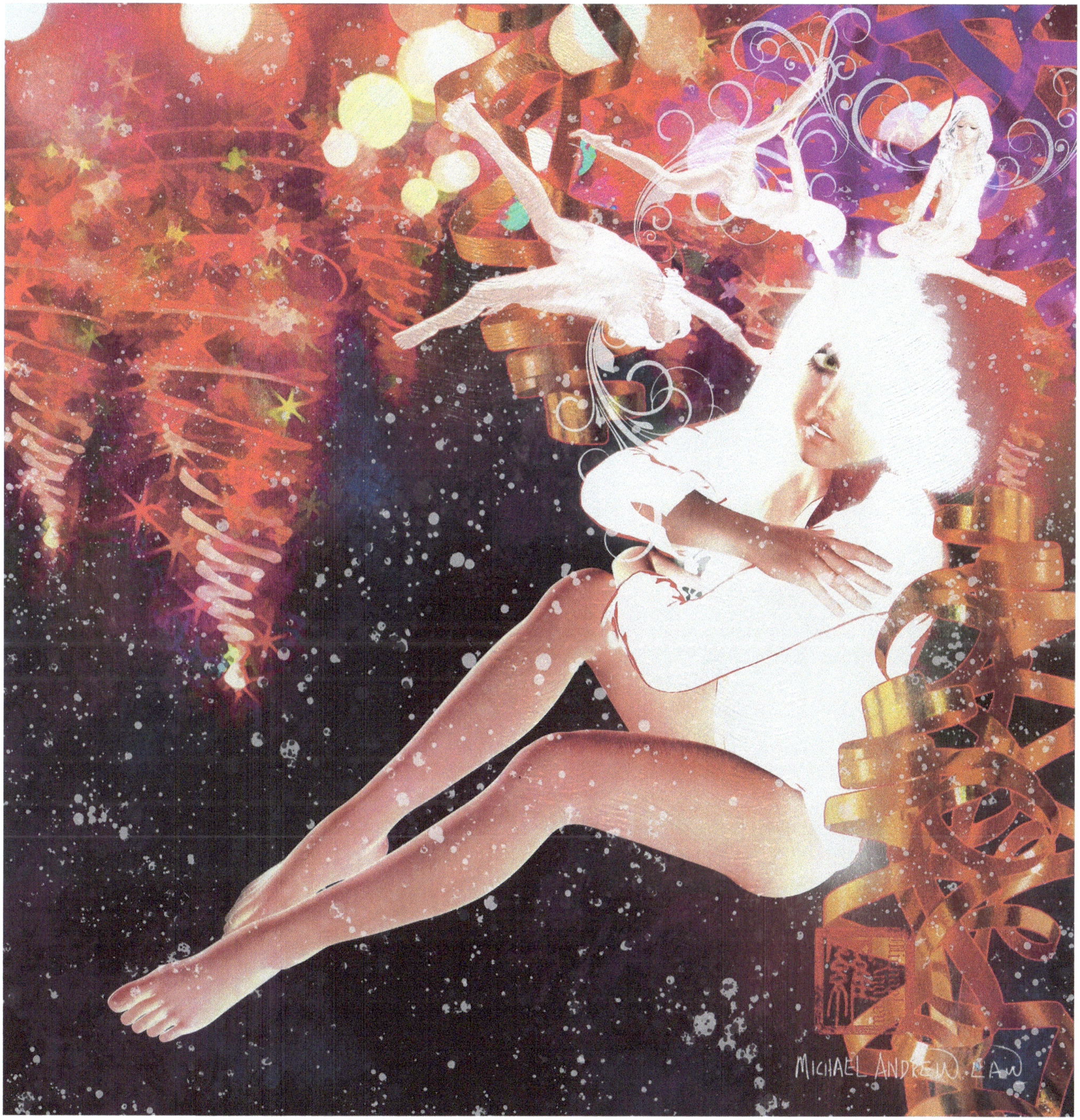

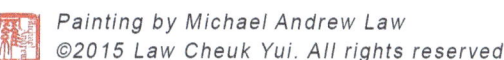

How all of our hopes Had come down to this child

Michael Andrew Law

(852) 6444-7550
info@michaelandrewlaw.com
www.michaelandrewlaw.com

Pale Hair Girls : iEgoism

Medium : Mixed Media Painting (oil and Acrylic) , Glitter , Gold Leaf .
About This Serie : Third Series of painting of The entire Pale Hair Girls Universe ,
done with mixed media on canvas , classical method crossover with contemporary painting method.
Number of Paintings : 960 (As of 2015)
Availability : Limited Edition , Prints , Special Edition .

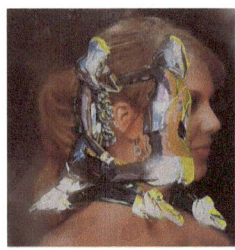
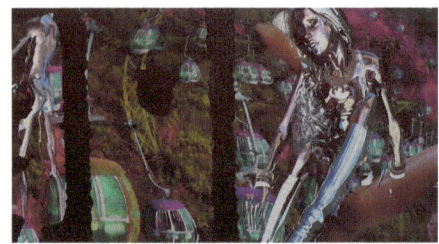

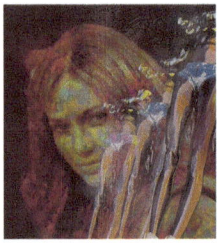
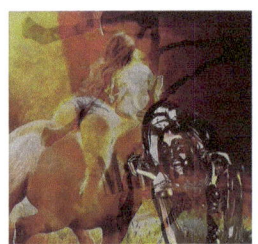
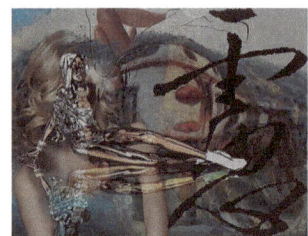

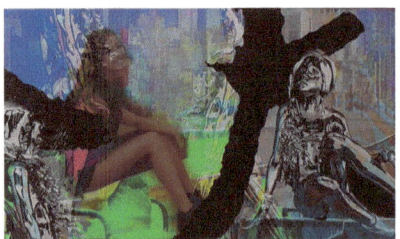
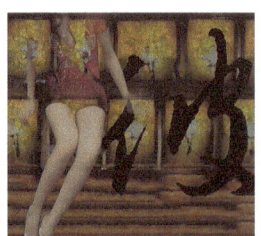

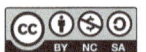

Michael Andrew Law

(852) 6444-7550
info@michaelandrewlaw.com
www.michaelandrewlaw.com

Pale Hair Girls : iEgoism

Medium : Mixed Media Painting (oil and Acrylic) , Glitter , Gold Leaf .
About This Serie : Third Series of painting of The entire Pale Hair Girls Universe ,
done with mixed media on canvas , classical method crossover with contemporary painting method.
Number of Paintings : 960 (As of 2015)
Availability : Limited Edition , Prints , Special Edition .

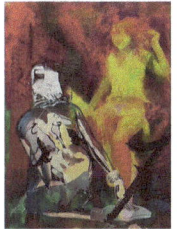
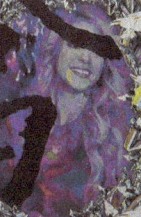
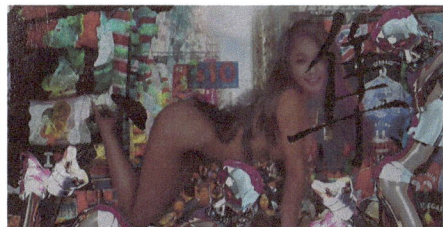

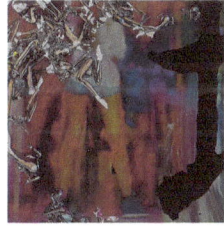
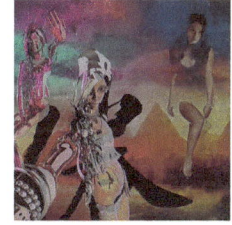
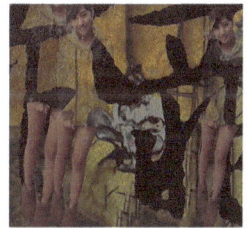

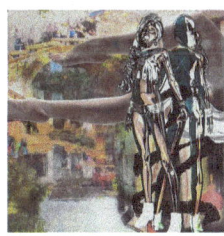
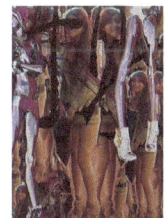
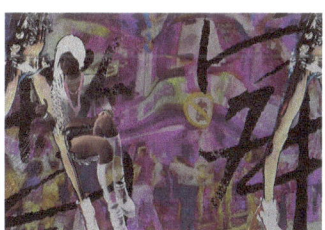

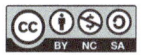

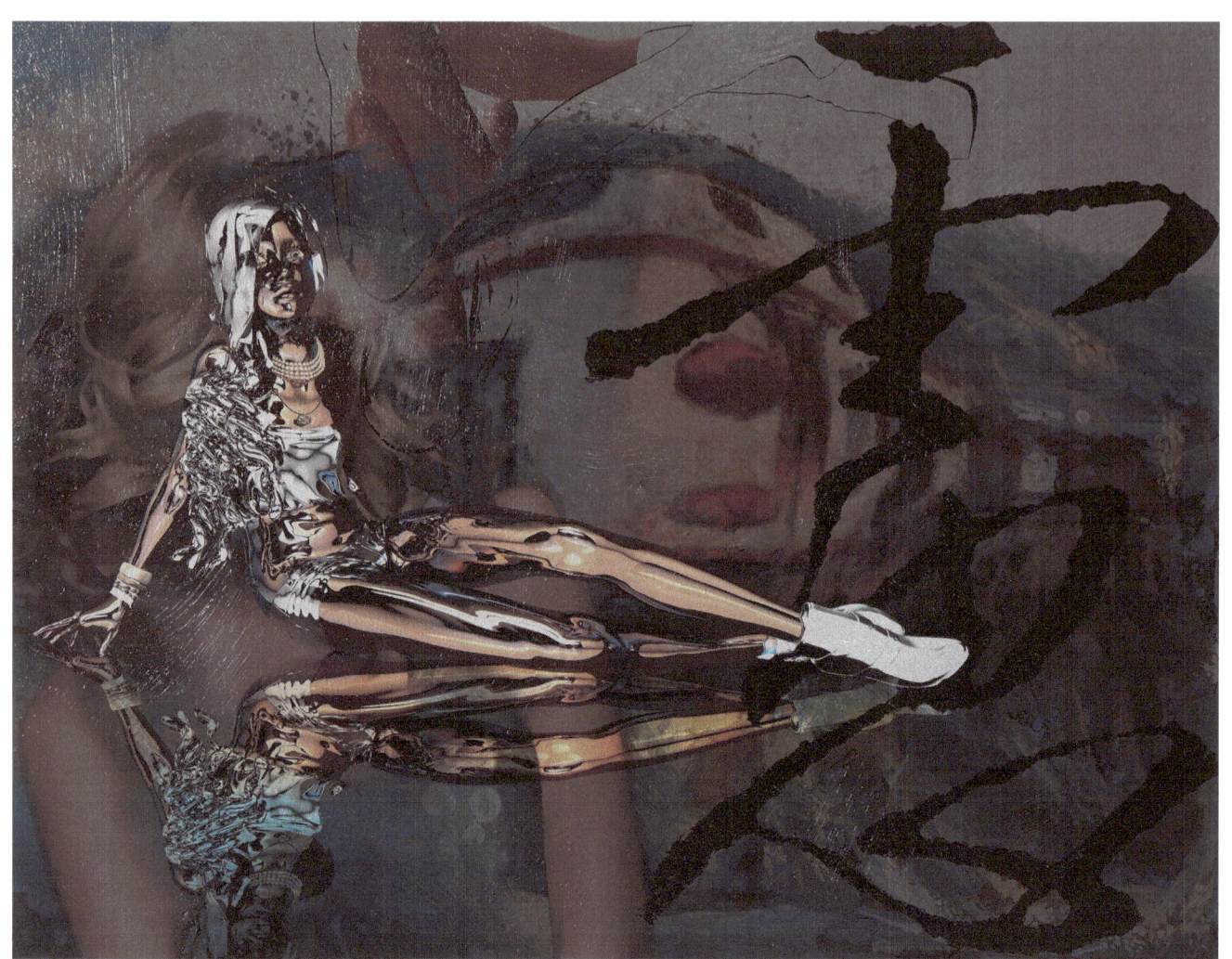

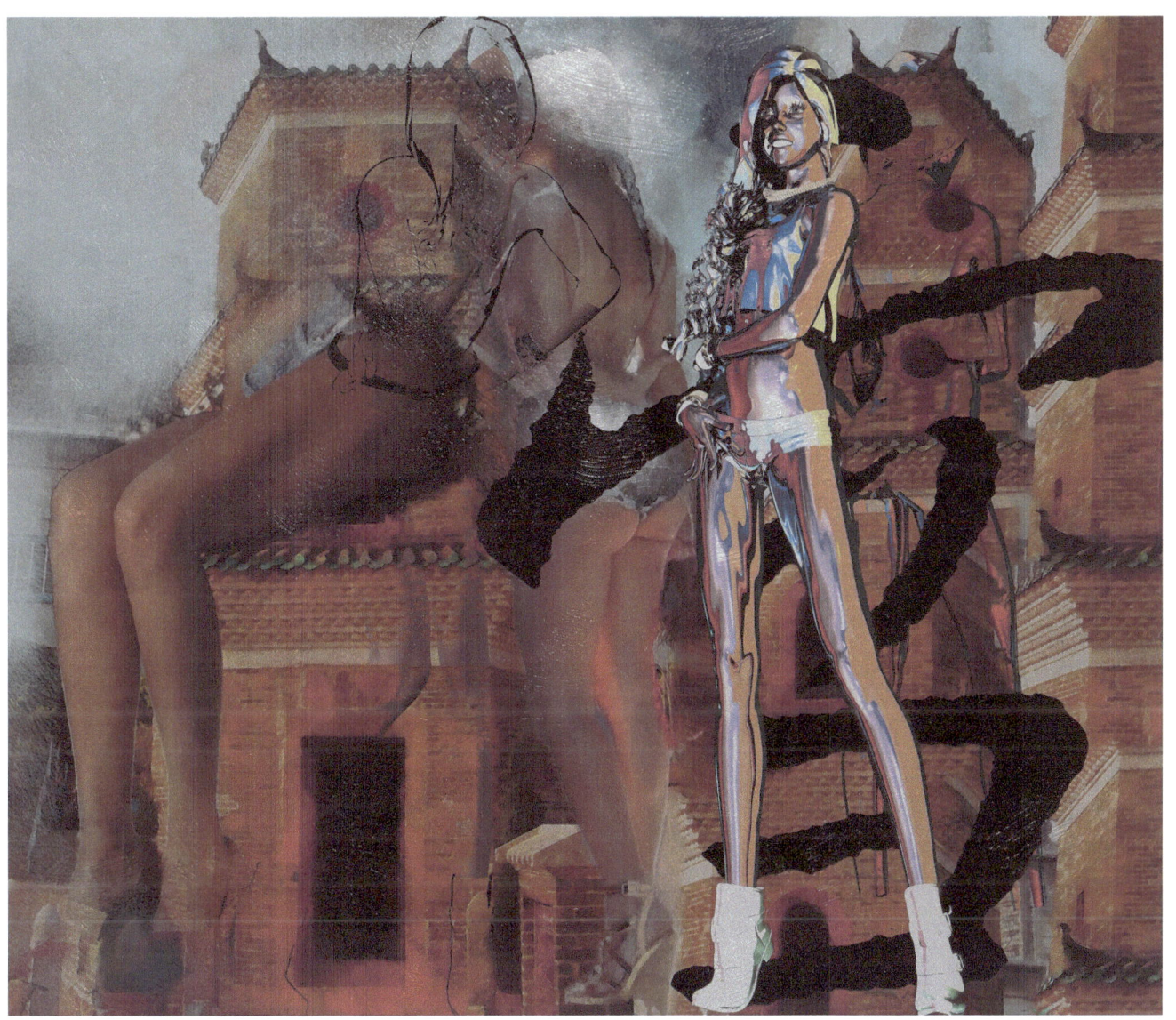

藝術家觀點：關於作品原創性及創新性

讀評論藝術家的作品時，原創性或新意等關鍵字經常也會被批評者提及；那麼究竟原創性或新意又是怎樣去量度呢？

首先，我可以較偏激點道，九成九九九的所謂100%原創作品是根本沒法生存下來。

我曾和一位要好的Hollywood獨立製片經理談劇本，他們一年會收到大約七千份劇本，是已寫好並已在公會註冊了的劇本，他會和助理去讀 [通常4頁左右拋掉的佔多]，這位獨立製片經理說，若你是寂寂無名的新人，若是自以為是不按既有hollywood的三段敘事模式而自創新方法，根本不會有機會過第一關 [被讀過3頁後丟掉]，他說首先不要太高估觀眾的領悟力，也不要低估既有模式的運作力，因為那是經過了一百年的驗證而hollywood仍然在生產著世界上最能要人掏腰包的電影圈子。

這個先不要怪甚麼制度扼殺創意，因為就如我先前所說的藝術界規則，藝術家必先在制度內生存下來，方法就只有在沿有的框框裏邊先賺點糊口錢，到你證明了你的能力，觀眾對你的所謂Track Record [有多次發表作品]有了信心後，才會開始有所謂接受「創意」的安全感；觀眾說不出這些因為安全感是空氣一樣，既重要但又不能缺乏。

若說明白點，就因為基本上若「創意」要生存下來只有兩種，能讓大眾一看即懂 [要做到「能讓大眾一看」已經很難，雖

已經很難， 雖說這個99%已經是既有之框框以內完成的創意]
，二是大眾一看卻未懂，但有一些「品牌評論人」去為那「創
意」作品「翻譯」[坦白點也叫「站台」] ，在這個情況下創
意空間也稍大 ，但你卻先要那「品牌評論人」對你的作品有安
全感[或鈔票感]。

若無以上兩項 ，任何再精彩之創意也只會隨即消失於這個只談
「錢」之社會上呢 ， 在藝術家的角度來說也許是聽來困難重
重 ， 但在回報的角度上看 ， 那些發了達的藝術家真的為人類
文明或精神上添了一點色彩 ， 才導致這麼多人去讀美術吧 ，
以為亂幹一通就能大賣 ， 最糟糕卻是現在的藝術在賣的「創
意」和在大學課堂理解的「創意」和大眾理解的「創意」各自
也不相同時 ，才會令很多年輕有志的藝術畢業生最後要轉行。
一，大眾看「藝術」則是用感覺去理解 ， 二，商業上在賣的
「藝術」是為了欺騙感覺去設計的 ， 三，在大學課堂理解的
「藝術」卻是為證明大學自我存在而設計的 ， 一和二者是很
快和粘在一起因為互相有需求關系 ， 三者卻在畢業後立刻發
覺不對路最後也要服從欺騙感覺這個模式。 [也就是所謂讀了
藝術是不會聰明了一點的說法 ，當然公道點說 ，大學作為藝
術理論和資料整合仍是有貢獻的，只是見過太多學生以為大學
畢業了就是向商業世界證明了自己的才幹。]

而說有關一個藝術家的作品上的演變[或順應文題叫再創新] ；
當然有很多例子的是藝術家創作時， 在偶爾的狀況發現新的方

法 ，就如Jackson Pollack ， 在創作時偶爾發現了滴畫的方法， 就去一直做了[只是即使Jackson Pollack 也是靠畫表現主義的作品由前半生支持到後期發現了滴畫才成名]，不過就如Chanel的設計師Karl Lagerfeld 曾說過 ，偶發的創意是不可倚靠的 ， 若然過了一年，2年3年，仍未能在偶爾的狀況發現比別人創造更具新意的方法又怎麼算 ？

所以更多的藝術家的作品是來自啟發自或取材自別人， 如畢加索也是個不甘於只沿用做過了的模式 ，但他卻不是偶爾發現了新的方法 ， 而是用去抄的-- 好聽的叫作引用別人的畫法 ， 這也不等如在貶低畢加索 ， 他是個極成功的藝術家 ， 在他的當代至現在亦有對他極好的評價 ， 即使他在生時亦早已承認了有抄的成份， 但亦毫不影響他在畫廊間的地位 ，即使討厭他的同輩或前輩甚至後輩再多。

即使現在也有極多例子的藝術家是用 引用別人 之方式去創作，例用國際間享負盛名師大編劇/導演 Quentin Tarantino ，Martin Scorsese 等 ， 他們便多次在作品引用他們欣賞的電影作品的元素 ，例如 港產片龍虎風雲 就 被認為是Quentin Ta-rantino 的成名作reservoir dogs 的基本引用素材 ， 然後Pulp Fiction 亦被指引用了 1963 年電影 Black Sabbath 的 編劇結構和Band of Outsiders 的視覺元素 等等 ； 再在這個模辦上再根據自己的喜好去作演繹 。

藝術創作上，很難用原創性作為一個指數去評斷 一份作品的價值 ； 再者 ，即使你的作品真的1000%是你的原創性也未必等於該作品能獲得重大成功－我所指的是商業上和口碑上的成功，那當然亦有運氣因素在內。但即使是要獲得專家點頭的認可，仍不是單單靠有原創性便行，反而若作品本身夠震憾或感動，仍是觀眾所需要的主要素，反而即使你真的是抄的，若讓你因種種原因而跑出了，仿間也只會認為你抄得好-抄得妙，久而久之，先到岸邊的就是皇者，也好難深究多少是原創，更極端的例子更是明明是抄了，靠此已岸上去[成功者也]的，即使有人深究，但已到岸上者早儲備了律師團，也不令欲深究者得逞已 [也不時看新聞道有其中懷疑有「被抄襲」之原著人或後人曾入稟索償，最後卻多數不了了之。]。

創作行業所謂的創作性說穿了就是如此。也許也不是全部亦不遠矣，若認真閱讀各藝術家，很難沒有前人的影子，即等如有說法「所有曲子也會有點莫札特的影子」，是事實還是誇張了？但哪幾個音符的組織等等樂理-這個框框便不是作為一個編曲可隨便用創意打破吧。也不是我能評斷；只是作為真正的創作人很快就會發現不用太過執著於原創兩個字，然而太過執著於原創性其實也是一種虛偽，因為即使觀眾欣賞的作品事後發現非100%原創，但重要的卻是作者要有眼光地選取素材去作辦，也是說把前人組成的框框加進自已的想法/方法，而然後再到作品本身的執行/製作上夠好，綜合得夠好而達到該概念或表現之目的，才是被認為一件成功和有價值的作品的準則，不過到最後，究竟某Designer 品牌的外衣突然大賣究竟是創新，還只是因為某A-List 被提名女星在奧斯卡典禮上穿著步紅地毯？

那套奧斯卡最佳影片是否「堅料」比另外二千多套同年出品的其他Hollywood電影優質和有新意呢，還只是因為投票的幾千位大製片，大演員或行內知己希望造一個新大王呢？

那隻被評論人驚為天人，Damien Hirst的鯊魚缸，又是否比那個比Damien Hirst早兩年把已鯊魚屍拿去展覽的Eddie Saunders的那個鯊魚更具有意念和品質呢？[還順帶一提Damien Hirst的鯊魚不是他本人捉，也不是他本人拿去浸缸，當然那個缸也不是他本人建的，反之早兩年的Eddie Saunders是自己捉的]

有時我也弄不清原創性及創新性這條究竟是該怎麼算的題。

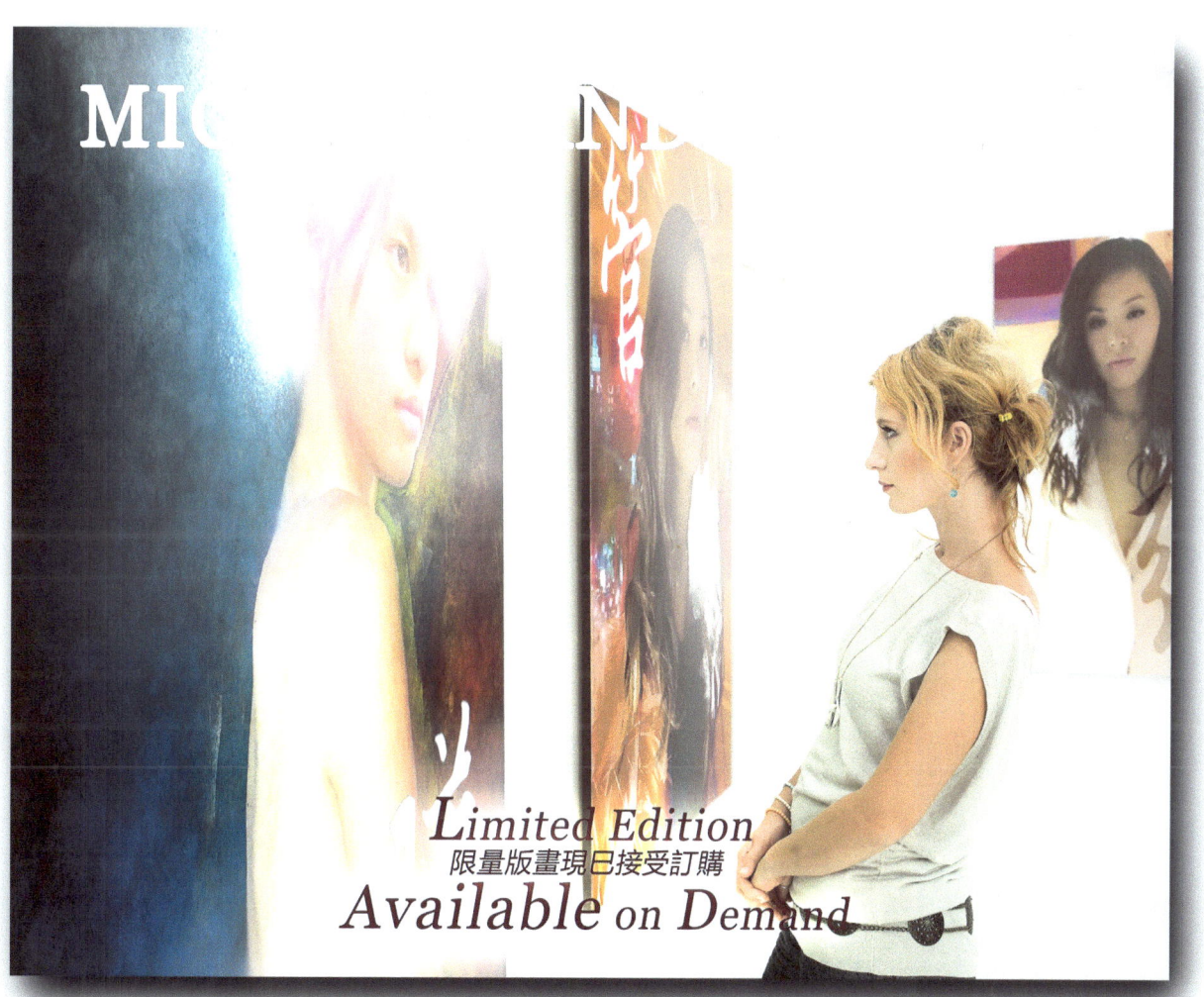

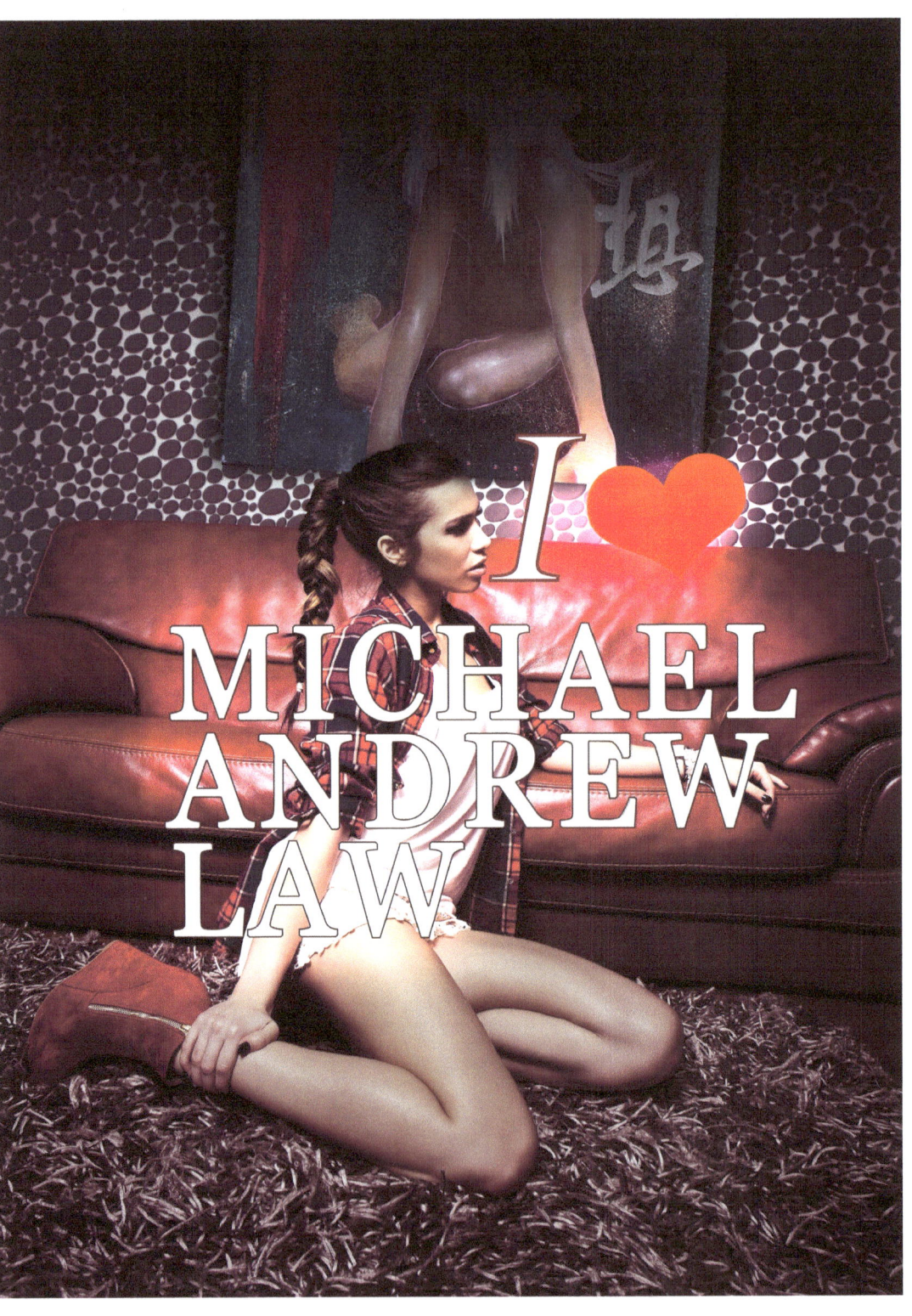

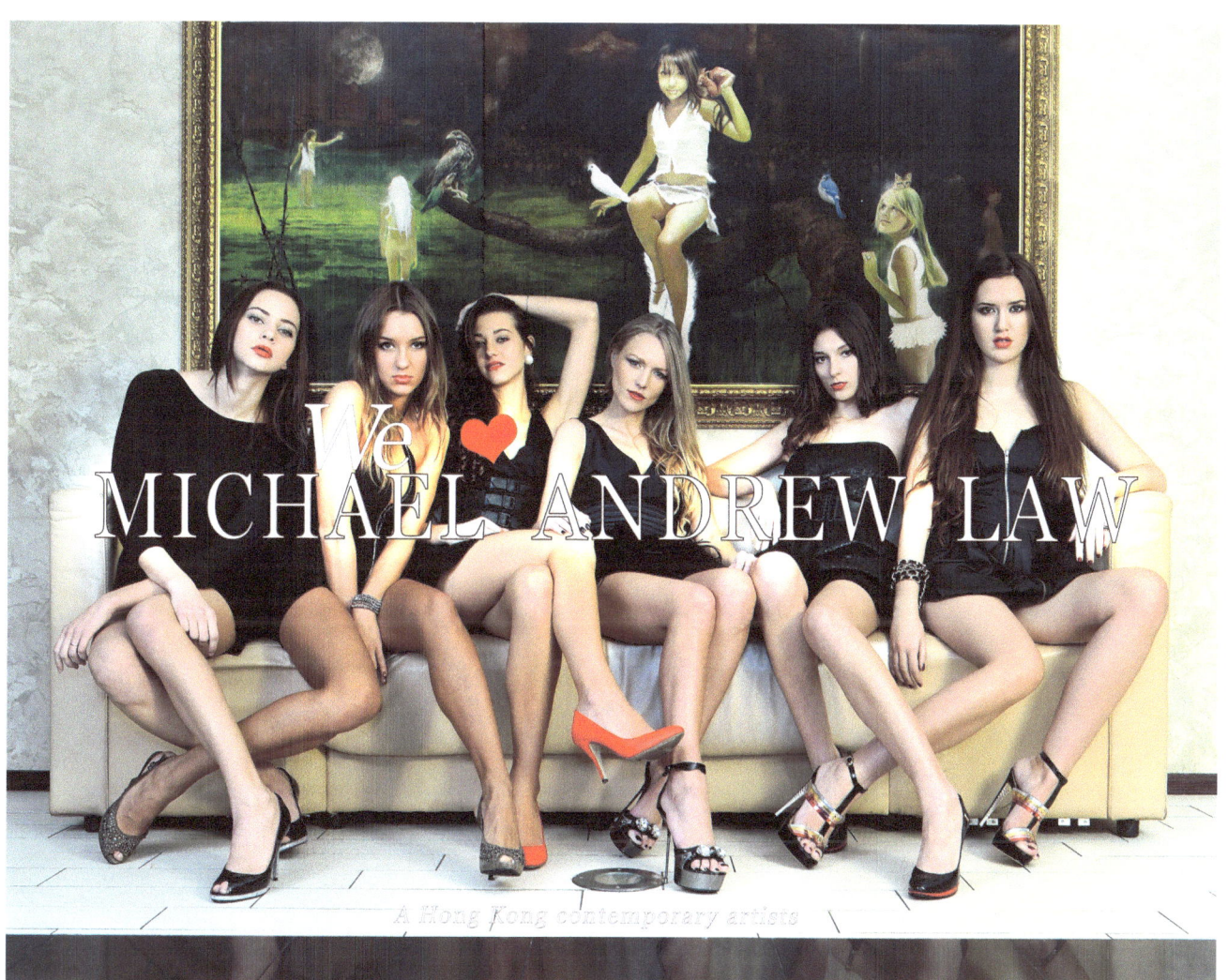

We ❤ MICHAEL ANDREW LAW

A Hong Kong contemporary artists

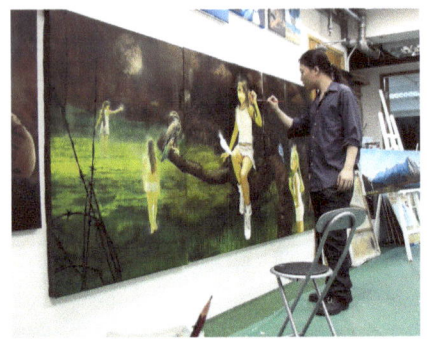

Michael Andrew Law at Work.

Michael Andrew Law fusing digital and classical painting with west and East creative philosophy , to produce an extremely original artistic language and content that bridged west and east ,classical and modern medium , at the same time clearly tells the stories of his own generation. Combining digital creative materials and classical painting techniques with effusive yet knowing and precise focused , his paintings maintain a powerful tension between opposing aesthetic forces—expression and knowledge, control and spontaneity, savagery and wit, urbanity and primitivism—while providing satiric commentary on the oppressive realities of the predicament of Generation Internet, homegrown hongkonger's local-culture vesus Traditional Chinese culture, and The Hong Kong's post-handover history.

In his dynamically designed compositions, gracefully detailed figures and innocent faces are incise against fields that juxtaposed with portraits, chinese calligraphy, and sometimes cgi. The Pale Hair Girls Series (2006 - 2013) depicts realistic cold, icy-like young female figures surrounded by abstract and expressively painted forms and shapes revealing images of Pop culture, Historial figures, and Hong Kong landmarks.

Michael Andrew Law draws inspiration from Old Master's works such as Caravaggio , Ruben , Rembrandt , all the way to the Modern Art Superstars such as Warhol , Lichtenstein , Richter , De Kooning , Bacon , Wool and Prince . The Pale Hair Girls series mainly inspired by the painting works of French academic painter and traditionalist William-Adolphe Bouguereau and the Late Great YiFei Chen's characteristic "Romantic Realism" paintings.

In a reversal of standard East-West aesthetics, Law re-interprets Old Master's sophisticated imagery combine classical and digital materials—which resonate with Digital Vector Designs and Paintings—with fine strokes of oil paint multi-layered with paint film.In his interpretation of Leonardo Da Vinci's iconic Mona Lisa's smile (1517)—an iconic image that has been endlessly disseminated and reproduced—Law painted over the symbolism of the portrait Mona Lisa with his young wife , intent on rendering the figure in contemporary fashion with the iconic image as background .

"The Humanity triptych" depicts New Generation HongKongers in a Ruined Hong Kong city , awaiting their unknown fate of a new beginning. This painting series explores one of the central paradox of his art—between romance and derision , his romantic magnanimity as an artist and his pessimistic perspective on the predicament of Generation Y Hongkongers. Here, this paradox is symbolized by the stark contrast of icy cold young female and disturbing representations of the armageddon-like of images. Whether portrayed as single "chinese calligraphy " or in triptych composition and classical paintwork that combine both expressive and traditional painting techniques with the digital vector , the beauties and the human figures stand as eternal motifs in the history of art and also in popular culture. Both oppositional and parallel, they are reminders of the fragile vibrancy of life and the impitoyable passing of time.

A references between different cultural refrence (high/pop, classical/contemporary, east/west), Michael Andrew Law has stated that an artist should be someone who understood how to hybrid between different worlds and go ahead makes an effort to knowing them. With his distinctive "iEgoism" philosophy , which employs highly refined academic painting techniques to depict a mixture of abstract expressionism within a representational pop culture images. These techniques parallel to the themes of romance and predicament of this generation , he recollects and revitalizes narratives of irony and introspection.

Michael Andrew Law was born in 1982 in British Hong Kong , studied fine art with american artist Daniel Anderson and with artist graduatee of China Central Academy of Fine Arts Sam Zeng from 2003 - 2006 . He co-founded the Hong Kong Art Studio Nature Art Workshop in 2008. In addition to the production and marketing of Michael Andrew Law's art and related work, Nature Art functions as a supportive environment for the
fostering of emerging Hong Konger artists. Law is also a curator. In 2013, he organized an exhibition of contemporary art titled "iEgoism ," which served as a commentaries of contemporary HongKong Gen Y pop culture ;These Theroy also published in the book : "ïEgoism" in 2014.

Michael Andrew Law currently works and lives in Hong Kong.

For further information please contact the studio at info@michaelandrewlaw.com or at +852.6444.7550. All images are subject to copyright. Artist/Studio/Gallery's approval must be granted prior to reproduction.

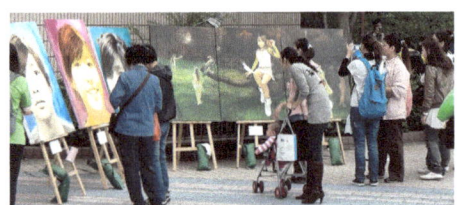
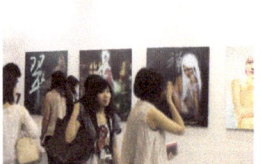

2010 Avenue of Stars, Hong Kong

Exhibition :

2013 DeTour Matters 2013 Satellite Events at NatureArt Gallery
2013 December to Remember , One man show at NatureArt Gallery Central District, Hong Kong.
2012 Solo Show , Park Central tseung kwan O ,Hong Kong
2011 Art Walk Group Showing , Discovery Bay ,Hong Kong
2011 HK Gold Coast (Book signing exhibition)
2009 Solo Painting Exhibition The Avenue of Stars
Group Exhibition of Daniel Anderson workshop Classical Realism class of 2008 at Manhattan,NY
2007 Guest and Exhibition The Peak Galleria Hong Kong
2007 Invited workshop exhibition, Elements, Hong Kong
Group Exhibition of Classical Realism class of 2007 at Manhattan,NY
2006 Collection by Cardinal Zen Ze-kiun and exhibited at Catholic Church of Hong Kong.
2004 - 2007, Hong Kong Young Artist Group Exhibition, Hong Kong Central Library.
Group Exhibition of Classical Realism class of 2006 at East Village, Manhattan,NY
2005 illustration original exhibition for Kung Kao Po
2004 Group Exhibition, Wanchai Tower
2003 Group Exhibition, Hong Kong Convention and Exhibition Centre,
2003 Winner of I luv Hong Kong Painting Competition, exhibition at The Landmark (Hong Kong).
2002 The Holy story Picture Book illustrated picture original exhibition ,sai wan ho civic centre.

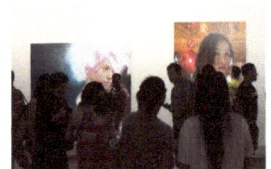

SELECTED COLLECTIONS :

Cardinal of the Catholic Church Joseph Zen Ze-kiun
Organic Beauty Inc
Agriculture, Fisheries and Conservation Department
Ms.Ho Wei Ying
Ms. Annie Yu
Daniel Anderson
MR.Tsang Yan Sam

PUBLICATIONS :

Fisheye magazine , featured artist interview , November 2002
Kung Kao Po , interview , June 2006
Art of Rock Realism , 2008
The Art of Michael Andrew Law , 2010
December to Remember One man Show Art Book , 2013
iEgoism , 2015

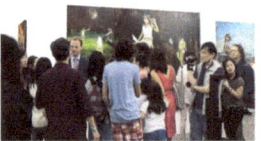

Solo Shows 2010 - 2013

I really appreciate your purchase of this Painting

Collection Book , I hope you enjoy reading them as

much as I enjoyed painting them!

May God bless your home with peace, joy and love.

From Michael Andrew Law.

Find Me Online.

Michael Andrew Law Q

www.ingramcontent.com/pod-product-compliance
Lightning Source LLC
Chambersburg PA
CBHW050827180526
45159CB00004B/1818